Application Hosting: Propelling Companies Forward

Running a server and maintaining an army of IT personnel is a big headache for most companies. Application hosting can solve these miseries so that management teams can devote more of their time on the business side of things and less on IT.

Basically, application hosting is a type of business process outsourcing. Application software and IT environments of companies will be remotely hosted by a third party application service provider. Companies opting for this service gain the advantage of reducing operational costs in maintaining a server, installation and maintenance of licensed software, and managing a full department of technology specialists.

Companies pay only for the use of business applications on a per-use basis or more commonly for a fixed monthly fee. Company financials can be easily managed because expense forecasts related to IT infrastructure are fixed for a set period.

Unforeseen budget disruption can also be eliminated if companies will take advantage of application hosting. Local server breakdowns or company-wide application crashes will definitely cause budget realignments because of costly repair or reinstallation. All of these misfortunes can be averted through remote application hosting.

A company can choose from a wide array of application service providers. This service has been in vogue for many years now. Companies who took advantage of this innovative technology gained an edge in terms of acquiring top of the line technology at minimum costs.

Saa
cess

ıc-
are

SaaS 100 Success Secrets

Copyright © 2008 by Gerard Blokdijk

SaaS 100 Success Secrets
Gerard Blokdijk

There has never been a SaaS manual like this.

100 Success Secrets is *not* about the ins and outs of a SaaS. Instead, it answers the top 100 questions that we are asked and those we come across in forums, our consultancy and education programs. It tells you exactly how to deal with those questions, with tips that have never before been offered in print.

This book is also *not* about a SaaS's best practice and standards details. Instead it introduces everything you want to know to be successful with SaaS.

Table of Contents

There is no doubt that information and communication technology is still the vehicle that propels businesses world wide. A company can get the best out of it through application hosting and software service providers.

Getting to Know Application Service Provider

Application service provider business is one of the best services that were spawned by modern Internet technology. Application service provider or ASP is a software solution model that virtually rents out application program technologies to numerous computer program consumers.

Application service providers use standard hypertext transfer protocol and HTML to distribute and deploy computer applications and software suites to end-users. In other words, consumers only need a computer, a standard web browser, and a reliable Internet connection in order to use specific programs for their computing needs.

An application service provider wholly owns the software or computer programs. End users will have to pay a fee for its use. Some application service providers charge clients monthly or annual payments for services rendered while others charge users whenever they use the service. In rare cases, ASPs may provide the service free for a certain period. Its a marketing tactic of some ASPs in order to get potential customers or to widen their client base.

Application service providers also maintain the necessary infrastructure to deliver the software to their clients. ASPs run and maintain their own powerful servers, provide customer support services, and they have their own technology specialists that keep the system running. Computer programs can be accessed by clients anywhere in the globe because ASPs provide the software through the Internet and can be accessed by account holders.

ASPs provide big help for start-up and small companies and convenience for large corporations. It can significantly lower the cost of every company's computing requirements.

ASP for Better Business Productivity

Working in the big business arena of software technology will mean locking horns with ASPs at some point in your career. But what is it, actually? ASP or application service provider is a business that provides services to customers in a computer-based network-efficient manner.

The software that is offered via an application service provider is usually called on demand software, or SaaS (software as a service).

Putting it in simpler terms, the business provides their customers and clients easy access to any particular application program they desire using HTTP as a standard protocol.

The demand for ASPs has slowly risen from its first introduction many years ago. It evolved from simply being a specialized software back in the day to the □go to guy□ of even small and medium scaled on line and web-based businesses now. Furthermore, the ever-increasing complexities of software have resulted in bigger costs in its distribution to the eagerly awaiting (and high paying) end users.

But thanks to application service providers, such complexities and high costs of this software can be bid adieu.

Additionally, the many issues regarding upgrading and enhancements have been eliminated by the end firms as well, firmly placing the responsibility of system management to the application service providers themselves, maintaining and making sure that services are up to date every hour of everyday (technical support) and ensuring physical and electronic security as well as built in support for more flexibility and seamless continuity of businesses.

It is no wonder that people are turning to ASPs for their business needs.

The ASP SAAS Business Model Explained

There are lots of acronyms today that are stirring the IT industry. Asp SaaS soa and what have you. To avoid confusion however, it should be noted that all of these refer to software services.

It is a business model where a service provider offers the use of a specific computer program to consumers using the Internet as the standard delivery vehicle. In simpler terms it means a provider rents the software to the consumer. The end user on the other hand pays a certain subscription fee to the service provider.

The more popular term for this business model though is SaaS or software as a service. Actually public utilities like electricity, air travel, and telephone services can be compared to SaaS. Consumers pay the services provided by an electric company or buy a ticket to get the services of an airline company.

The reason is common sense because it would be very impractical and expensive for a consumer to buy an airplane and maintain it just to fly back home or go to a business trip.

The analogy is perfect for software services. A company will have to build their own IT environment, maintain the server, hire technicians and experts, buy expensive software, install it on main frames, deploy it on a LAN, etc.

These would be very expensive, time consuming, and sure sources of big headaches. Software service providers offer to solve this by using their own servers to deploy the computer program to the consumer. It virtually rents out the software and the user only needs a PC and an Internet connection.

SaaS business model is a win-win solution for the service providers and end users. The customer cut their IT costs while their subscription to the service increases the income of software service providers.

The Many Benefits of SaaS

SaaS also known as Software as a Service, provides convenience to both customers and clients. Software companies today believe that the on-demand software applications are the wave of the future and will totally eradicate traditional business software. Many SaaS companies produce applications are now being sold as a service that is paid as-needed. The benefits of SaaS is that it is a web-based service that focuses solely on the customers' needs. The basic secret of their success is that they practice the principle of being a consumer based web company rather than a software company.

There are several benefits of SaaS over the traditional enterprise model software applications. First, the customers have the ability to provide feedback for buggy software. There are even applications that automatically give the host feedback on customer usage of the application. The software company is therefore held accountable for bug fixes and updates.

Second, the SaaS company is more customer-focused and customer-friendly. This means that any SaaS software is made available for the customer to easily set it up without the hassles of finding technical crews to install it for them.

Another one of the benefits of SaaS is that the cost of investing on the software is not that high. Customers can easily set up a monthly or yearly subscription for the software and can easily end it with just a simple click of a mouse. There is no need for a large sum of money in order to avail of the service.

The most important of all the benefits of SaaS is probably the frequent and easy updates of the software. Bug fixes are easily resolved and customers are assured that they constantly get the best version of their software.

Do I Need Collaborative SaaS Solutions for My Business?

Let us clarify first that collaborative IT solutions are simply IT solutions that help people who work for different parts of a large enterprise (such as different departments) or in different geographic locations (such as in different cities) to collaborate on a certain project.

Collaborative SaaS is one type of collaborative IT solution, meaning that small- and medium-sized businesses can use SaaS via the Internet to keep external and internal members of a project in constant communication with one another.

There are a few key rules that companies opting for collaborative SaaS should consider.

First, collaborative SaaS solutions should be as simple as possible to allow more companies to adopt collaborative SaaS.

Collaborative SaaS should also grow better and faster if there are more individuals and corporations opting to use collaborative SaaS.

Second, if your company is opting for collaborative SaaS, then start out your endeavor with a browser-based SaaS solution first. Small- and medium-sized businesses can even transfer their value network into the service when required.

Third, you may find that collaborative SaaS vendors might amend an earlier solution provided or provide new and better solutions.

Fourth, it is more advisable for collaborative SaaS companies to avoid the horizontal market (where the bigger collaboration players tend to congregate) and just target their collaborative SaaS efforts at the vertical market instead. So if you are looking for a collaborative SaaS vendor to patronize, it would be wise to contact resellers or channels to get the best deals.

How CRM Matches Up to Other Sectors of the SaaS Market

CRM is usually seen as the biggest shareholder of the ever growing market sector of software as a service (or SaaS), but this does not mean that is the singular dominating body.

If the trend performance pushes through the way it is progressing right now, we might very well see Crm lagging behind the newfangled sectors of computer software that are all dead set on adopting the software as a service model.

One particularly fiery section of this is compliance management.

Compliance management is now considered to be the second largest marketing segment in software as a service, that is, according to most researches done in the biggest and most powerful business capitals around the world.

To add to Crm's woes, other functional areas such as procurement, enterprise resource planning, document management and e-commerce are also being presented and delivered as on-demand services.

There seem to be many reasons as to why compliance management is very well suited to such a delivery model.

To begin with, the regulations are always undergoing changes, so it is necessary to upgrade one's system each time such a change happens. Such a model is considered to be a highly superior alternative to the usual solutions.

Currently, the Crm on demand sector is showing weak signs of being adopted in a mature market phase. As the signs point out, something needs to be done - perhaps a total revolution of the CRM system, or a system and implementation redesign - soon in order to remedy this.

How to Define SaaS

Software as a service or SaaS goes by many names. It is also called hosted application, application service provider, hosted solutions, and a lot more. These terms however only mean one thing: SaaS is a method of delivering a computer program to users using the Internet. This could well be the simplest definition of software as a service or SaaS.

To elaborate further, software as a service means that the computer application being used by the customer is hosted remotely using the servers and infrastructure of the service provider. The service could include a single application or a suite of different applications. Data storage is also provided by the SaaS company as well as the necessary technical support and maintenance of the program.

The customer on the other hand must subscribe to the service. A regular fee is paid monthly, annually or in some cases on a pay per use basis. The customer should also possess a computer console, a web browser and a reliable Internet connection.

Upon payment of the subscription fee, the customer can instantly use the program. The service provider on the other hand is responsible in delivering fast uptimes, prompt technical support, and regular upgrades and patches to avoid bugs and software glitches.

This software service business model is getting popular among start up businesses and small industries. SaaS can provide cheap computing solution and total flexibility on software use which is very important for modern businesses and enterprises. Information about SaaS abounds on the Internet and these could be very helpful in guiding the customer in choosing the best SaaS provider.

The EMC SaaS Business Strategy

EMC became interested in venturing into the SaaS business because it knows it has many solutions in the backup and archiving field which may be evolved into SaaS solutions as well. Basically, EMC wants the SaaS solutions to serve as a complement for the low-end storage solutions EMC will also be offering. EMC is opting for these markets because in the past EMC did not serve the SaaS and low-end storage markets effectively enough.

If EMC does manage to delve into SaaS, it will have to fully address any pricing issues which have bogged down SaaS initiatives in the past (particularly with regards to metering plus cost transparency issues.) The problem hinges on the fact that SaaS pricing changes depending on usage.

The plan by EMC to venture into the SaaS business seems to follow a business trend where storage solutions vendors are tapping into the SaaS field as well, as part of their expansion efforts. Right now, EMC is the seventh-biggest player in the enterprise software business.

EMC recognizes that SaaS is a competitive alternative to the traditional way that software has been developed and marketed. Usually, software was built up to be always licensed as a model which was beneficial to traditional software companies. Rather than deal with SaaS a threat, EMC would rather consider SaaS as a business opportunity presented to them to accept and develop further.

One way EMC has been able to enter the SaaS arena is with its October 2007 purchase of Berkeley Data Systems which makes online backup service Mozy. This is also the path being taken by other vendors who are interested in competing in SaaS.

Enterprise SaaS: Venturing into the Big League

For many years enterprise SaaS or the adoption of software as service technology to enterprise-wide operations has been smirked at by IT experts and CEOs alike. But advances in the development of software and improvement of delivery infrastructure have led many executives in taking a second look at SaaS as a useful tool for their businesses.

As a newly flourishing industry, software as a service was not taken seriously by large traditional corporations.

The most that they can give to SaaS are small redundant operations which are not vital company functions. However, the success of many SaaS based companies created a buzz which industry leaders could not ignore. The increasing functionality of SaaS applications has become evident as technology develops.

SaaS companies specifically developed software that can be used by an enterprise. This is good foresight on the part of SaaS companies in order to entice large enterprises to take the SaaS route.

Today, there are software service answering the need for such vital enterprise functions like inventory control and management, company financials, procurement and dispatch, and many more. SaaS companies have elevated their level of sophistication in deploying software that can be very useful for different enterprise.

Software as a service is a new technology innovation. Its use in big corporations has just been starting.

But the potential of enterprise SaaS to deliver the necessary program for established corporation is already there. It could be a matter of time only when even large organizations and big enterprises will adopt the technology offered by SaaS.

The Lowdown on Erp Benefits

ERP or enterprise resource planning is a set of systems that attempt to unify all data information and processes of a particular organization into one cohesive system.

Your usual ERP system will make full use of multiple parts of a computer software and hardware in order to make this integration happen. One vital element of most enterprise resource planning systems includes the use of a unified storage database in order to create an archive of all the data of different modules of the system.

The enterprise resource planning system is very important for any organization.

Without it, a company might find itself with a multitude of software applications that do not sync up with one another, thus leading to a failure in effective interface. These different software applications have many tasks to fulfill, such as figuring out the best way to manufacture a particular product (design engineering), managing the tracking forms of all the orders, ensuring the efficient system of revenue cycles, and managing and merging the interdependent bill of materials.

Enterprise resource planning has several security features that are embedded in its system.

This is necessary in order to protect the system against crimes like industrial espionage, as well as outside/inside jobs like embezzlement. The security feature of enterprise resource planning includes a data tampering protection in the event that a discontent employee intentionally tries to modify the prices of the products so as to contribute the demise of the company, or other such types of plans of sabotage. The enterprise resource planning systems provide great functionality in order to implement more internal controls so as to prevent actions like this.

Microsoft Hosted Sharepoint, Taking File Sharing to a New Level

Collaboration is the term that best describes the concept behind Microsoft Sharepoint Services. Sharepoint is a kind of software developed by Microsoft that can be used to host web sites that makes it possible for users to access shared information, documents, records and any other forms of applications through a browser. These Sharepoint sites are actually ASP.net applications that are made up of web parts, which are then added to form web pages. These are configured by site users and administrators to create a complete web-based application and then hosted in the portal of Sharepoint. The unified Sharepoint platform offers advantages for team community, and individual empowerment.

From the word itself □sharepoint□, you can determine more or less what it is about. It means that sharing of information, documents, and individual ideas are captured on Sharepoint sites to facilitate cooperation and participation among team members. The content on these sites can be viewed on any web browser, making it more accessible to users.

What□s good about using Sharepoint is that site members can communicate with experts and contacts via instant messaging or email. Site content can be personalized while ensuring that site members have the right access to relevant information. Users can even receive alerts once new information or documents become available or changes are made to existing ones. Site content can be searched easily as well, and some web parts can be presented to a targeted audience only. Aside from these, rest assured that organization wide standards are still being met, especially when it comes to security and data integrity. Wikis and blogs are just two of the most common specialized applications that work well with Share-point.

Hosted Applications: Giving Birth to Virtual Companies

The increasing number of companies that use the Internet and the use of broadband technologies for high speed connections opened the way for hosted applications to make significant headway in the software industry.

Hosted applications are computer programs or software which can be used without installing it on local servers or individual PCs. Users only need an Internet browser and reliable connection in order to use and access the software.

These hosted applications are owned by application service providers and they use their own servers and hardware infrastructures to deliver the software to consumers. Users pay the ASPs whenever they utilize the software. Sometimes, a fixed monthly or annual fee is charged for the use of applications.

This model eliminates the need to install additional hardware or drive space to run the program.

Because the program uses web interface, users can use it when they want to and wherever they are. The technology is a big help in reducing the cost of IT requirements of companies. It can eliminate big investments for powerful IT environments.

Hosted application also contributes to the increasing flexibility of company operations.

Computing can be achieved even if employees work at different locations. Employees only need to access the company's account in order to use the necessary program. This will cut the cost of maintaining a centralized office.

Hosted applications are ideal for a company that wants to operate with minimum overhead capitalization. In fact this kind of technology can spawn virtual companies that operate primarily in cyberspace.

Taking Care of Customers through Hosted CRM

In order to succeed, businesses should have exemplary customer relationship management or crm. However, the prohibitive costs of maintaining good customer relations work force often results to sacrificing this aspect of the business. A superior alternative that businesses can adopt is hosted crm.

Hosted crm can provide effective and at the same time cost efficient customer relation services. Hosted crm applications can significantly increase performance of companies in terms of sales improvement, customer satisfaction, and after-sales follow up. Having a good customer relationship management service by way of hosted crm can boost a company's profitability and market performance.

Hosted crm will require minimum effort on the part of companies. A computer and reliable Internet connection are the only tools needed and companies can start their crm service immediately. Top of the line crm providers offer clients flexibility of use. This means that client companies subscribing to a hosted service have the option to customize their crm service according to specific needs.

Full automation of crm services can be programmed in order to answer the needs of potential and existing customers. This only shows the advantages of hosted crm especially before and after sales transactions. Hosted crm can also be customized to encourage repeat purchases.

Today, not only start up and small businesses are taking advantage of hosted crm. Even industry moguls and big corporations are shifting their customer relations desk to hosted crm services. It is a clear signal that hosted crm can bring lots of benefits to a company□s customer relation work.

The Advantages of Getting Hosted Software

Hosted software is business concept where a service provider rents out a specific computer program to companies or individuals. This can unburden end users of paying stiff licensing fees for commercial software use.

It will also be convenient for customers to opt for hosted software because it does not require costly hardware infrastructure. A client only needs a computer desktop and an internet connection and the software can be used almost immediately.

Hosted software has been in the market for several years already. But it gained popularity in recent years primarily because companies want to streamline their software solution deployment. Hosted software also benefits companies operating on a wide network.

Through hosted software, the need for a cumbersome computing facility has been eliminated and companies can enjoy the flexibility of computer applications accessible over the Internet.

A service provider offering hosted software can also provide unlimited storage and data archiving services for their clients. This component service unclogs the information overload of companies which is a big headache for most company information officers.

Hosted software companies also have their own technical support staff to maintain flawless running of applications and to provide glitch free processing of business solutions and data. Companies can now lower their cost of maintaining redundant services such as the upkeep of servers and software maintenance.

The potential of hosted software in giving companies complete computing benefits has been proven to work. This is the reason why application service providers are gaining renewed vigor in the IT market.

IDC SaaS Outlook: The Future is Bright

The International Data Center or IDC is a technology based institution that provides strategic analysis of technology issues, market studies on the IT sector, and investment intelligence for businesses.

IDC conducts in-depth research on emerging trends on technologies that may impact on business decisions and repositioning. Recently, IDC has studied the impact of SaaS business model on partner industries and shows which direction this new technology is going. It also studied the impact of SaaS adoption and recommendations have been proposed for this specific technology sector.

The study of IDC showed the increasing trend on aggressive expansion of SaaS companies in order to reach their development goals. The expansion of SaaS is propelled by the increasing growth of the market. In effect, SaaS companies are fast tracking their growth rates in order to match the market demands.

It is believed that to reach target growth rates, SaaS companies must strengthen its partnerships with subscribers. The IDC showed that this will be the key factor in sustaining the growth and expansion of the SaaS business model.

Notice was also given to the fact that SaaS providers should improve strategic outlook in future software development. To achieve optimum customer satisfaction, SaaS vendors must emphasize the development of technology focusing primarily on the business processes side rather than on technology.

The future is bright for the SaaS model and companies offering this type of software service. Growth has been noted and its sustainability is anchored on continued software development that is more business centered.

Microsoft SaaS, How to Apply for the Microsoft SaaS On-Ramp Program

If you are an independent software vendor (ISV) and you are planning to distribute software applications via the internet through Software as a Service (SaaS), then you may want to consider applying for the Microsoft SaaS On-Ramp Program.

Taking advantage of this program will make it easier for you, as an ISV, to market your own SaaS application.

Once you have registered and licensed the software using the Microsoft Services Provider Licensing Program or SPLA, you can then enjoy the such benefits that include the following:

(a) Special price offered on Windows and SQL servers for a year;

(b) Flexible licensing model without any commitments or upfront software costs: and

(c) Access to additional Microsoft technical, development, marketing and testing resources.

But then again, some program requirements need to be completed such as the following:

(a) A maximum configuration of eight Windows Server CPUs and two SQL Server CPUs can be licensed at a special rate;

(b) ISVs must have their own intellectual property for the SaaS application;

(c) ISVs must obtain a signed Microsoft Services Provider Licensing Agreement (SPLA), which enables ISVs to gain access to a number of Microsoft products and will then be used to provide services and applications to customers; and

(d) ISVs must be a Microsoft Partner Program registered member. To register as a member of the Microsoft Partner Program, ISVs must enroll in Microsoft Empower for ISVs. However, it would be best if ISVs must become a Certified or Gold Certified Partner with ISV/Software Solutions Competencies to make the most out of a working relationship with Microsoft.

The MIT SaaS Model: Education for All Using SaaS

SaaS or software as a service is commonly used in businesses. Actually the core target of SaaS companies and providers are enterprises which need an open source application deployable in different locations and environments. SaaS has provided this service and answered a particular market need. It has contributed greatly to the success of most SaaS companies and providers offering similar technologies.

The SaaS model uses the Internet to provide computer applications to companies. This computer program is readily available anytime from any part of the globe. A similar technology has been initiated by the prestigious Massachusetts Institute of Technology or MIT. A SaaS type model has been launched similar to the principles of delivery and service of the SaaS model. However, the MIT SaaS does not follow profitability goals of SaaS companies. This is because the institution primarily devotes its services for the benefit of knowledge itself.

MIT experts developed software called OpenCourseWare or OCW. It is similar to other open source software and is also readily available using only the Internet. Use of the SaaS-type MIT software is free and its target audience are educators, students, researchers, and distance learning institutions. OCW mimics the principle of the SaaS model because it can be accessed through the web and instantly available to users. It could be termed as hosted educational software where archived data and materials are stored remotely on MIT servers and it could be accessed by anyone around the globe.

The MIT SaaS shows that the technology behind SaaS can be used not just for business purposes but also for other non-profit and educational services.

Software As A Service (SaaS) : An Introduction to On Demand Applications

Customer satisfaction is always the goal of companies offering products and services to the public. Because of this, business owners always seek for new ideas and concepts, making life a lot more convenient than the usual. Say for example AOL, which is a well known brand when it comes to providing on demand applications to its members. Such exclusives are provided to different people with various interests and needs.

These include music videos, movie trailers and concert live feeds for entertainment fanatics, and call features like call alerts, voicemail and VOIP for office personnel.

This concept is also the same with Software as a Service (SaaS), wherein an on demand application is hosted on a remote server by a service provider and made available through the internet.

There are two major categories of SaaS and these are line of business services and customer-oriented services. The only difference lies on the target market on which these are being offered to.

Line of business services is being offered to companies and enterprises such as customer relations applications and management programs, while customer-oriented services are open to the general public such as web-based email. Both are being offered for free, though customer-oriented services can also be used for free.

An on demand software application delivered by SaaS has the following key characteristics. First, it is network-based and is commercially available. Second is that every activity done are being managed from centralized locations, making it possible for customers to access applications anytime anywhere over the internet. And lastly, there is no need for downloadable upgrades and patches because of centralized feature updating.

On demand (and On the Go!)

With everyone hot in pursuit of software as a service (or SaaS), it is very easy to see how exciting such a time might be for business providers and end users alike □ most especially in the sector of on demand services.

This on demand service can be seen as a solution or a special feature that is able to address the need of the user for instant results and efficient control of solutions. In a lot of cases, the value proposition of such a service is all rolled up in the fact that the end user or service client is seen to avoid a particularly significant financial investment. Instead, he or she participates in a scheme that includes the popular □pay as you go□ method. This scheme has done much to increase the popularity and utility of on demand service because of its value of affordability.

On demand services have a lot to offer for the eager consumers. It has video on demand, which is a special type of service that allows all the viewers to have access their media once they have subscribed to it, including PPV television offerings and streaming internet. It also offers on demand computing, often called utility computing, and presents a service where the software itself can process the transaction upon subscription. In such a model, the software is not really installed at the device of the user □ the way to work it is to access it via Internet or at a centralized access point. Such a software is usually delivered by an ASP and is usually referred to as software as a service.

On Demand SaaS: A Brief Back-grounder

On demand SaaS is no different from software service, hosted application, and software on demand. These are all business models offering software as a service. This kind of service uses modern Internet technology to deploy a wide array of computer application to customers. There is a global market for this service because the application, using web protocols, can be accessed anywhere as long as the customer has Internet connection.

The history of SaaS is a bumpy one. It experienced set back because the software market did not received it well. In the last decade, SaaS technology was on its infancy and customers expected more from the service. Market expectations could not be met by the service providers and it resulted to failures and closures of early SaaS companies.

With the advent of new technologies and increasing sophistication of software development, SaaS providers experienced a rebound and this time the market has responded positively. The synergy between software vendors and IT infrastructure providers has led to the development of more reliable IT environments and cutting-edge software. Expectations were met and growth of this particular sector has been increasing ever since it returned to the market.

Today, businesses are taking advantage of the benefits of SaaS. It significantly lowered the operational expenses of companies and provided perfect software solution for their computing requirements. More companies now have been migrating to SaaS enablement from the traditional in-premise software deployment.

The trend is going towards further growth and it is expected that service providers will refine their solutions as the sector develops.

On Demand Software: Surging Ahead to Meet Global Needs

The changing nature of how corporations operate has led to changes in software needs and utilization. The increasing dispersal and outsourcing of vital corporate functions and the popularity of virtual offices made in-house software and server environments obsolete. That is why there is a renewed market surge for on demand software.

On demand software is a service offered by application service providers. It is a business model in which a specific computer program can be made available to customers on a per use basis. Simply said, customers can lease a software which they can access anywhere because the mode of delivery only uses standard Internet protocols.

On the part of customers, on demand software is a big money saver. Businesses can do away with expensive on-site servers and costly software installations and maintenance. They also get operational flexibility because diverse departments located separately can still function as a unified unit because of the ability to access data from the service provider□s server. Virtual offices can be set up and workers can telecommute and work from their home. This can significantly slash company overhead and minimize problems concerning IT maintenance and support.

On demand software is really becoming the hottest buzz in the corporate world. The advantages of using the system far outweigh its disadvantages. That is why software as a service model has been gaining lots of adherents. In fact even multinational and big corporations are shifting their focus on software as a service. It

is viewed as the ultimate software solution to efficiently interconnect large organizations at very minimal cost.

Open source SaaS, Timely Realizations About Open Source SaaS

Almost every single tech enthusiast and online business guru is singing songs of praises, for open source SaaS is finally here. Come to think of it, it actually has been here for quite some time now.

It is just that it is only now that people are realizing its meaning and significance in the world of online communication and business □ even though we have been using web-based open source applications for years!

One main consideration of open source SaaS is its ability to help you wield better control over your many work and web-based applications. Can you assess how much of the stuff you have on your computer, the stuff that makes you do the things you do, is all part of the spirit of what people call the open source SaaS movement? You may be surprised to know that the answer is, more often than not, a resounding yes.

Open source SaaS is different from a lot of SaaS service providers. A lot of the 'others' out there have really good online distributions of their applications, allowing you to have great functionality in a web-based environment.

But do these other SaaS applications permit you to access the pages that control your graphic user interface? Do they allow you to access the database so that you may edit its contents? Through these other applications, are you able to control the file and the structure of the directory of your web applications? The hanging question is: are you totally in control? After mulling over these questions and realizing that only open source SaaS can provide you with significant browser functions in order to customize your productivity levels, it is most likely that you will see where you can make up for your years of lost gains, by investing in open source SaaS!

Opsource: Giving SaaS a Needed Shot in the Arm

The opsource SaaS enablement and delivery method bridges the gap between independent software vendors and end user software consumers. Opsource provided the necessary infrastructure that enabled software developers to effectively market their product solutions to a wider customer base at reduced cost.

The business model allowed software vendors to focus their efforts in developing top of the line software solutions without investing on expensive software delivery architecture.

Opsource provided the service to be the main vehicle in delivering software products to customers. This resulted to cheaper software which is readily available for interested subscribers. This is one of the main reasons why software as a service continues to enjoy competitive market edge in terms of pricing and quality.

Software as a service is not a new business model. In fact, it has existed long before the Internet became the number one source of information and services. Early SaaS models encountered difficulties in the market.

Because of increasing cost in setting up and maintaining a reliable software delivery system, application service providers sacrificed the quality of software development in order to meet the demands of running their own delivery infrastructure. These resulted to cold market reception which led to the early ASP downfall.

The opsource model reversed everything. SaaS now is enjoying renewed market vigor and ultimate dominance in the software industry. This is due to the fact that software vendors can now concentrate on creating cutting edge software technologies which are very useful to end consumers. Developers have been unburdened of expensive hardware maintenance. It kept the prices of exceptional software low and the market received it positively.

Opsource SaaS : Affordable meets Functional in one Value-Packed software

It is a very exciting time in the world of software as a service or SaaS, for the time has come for Opsource SaaS to shine! Touted as the delivery experts,

OpSource is determined to provide its customers with the necessary operational infrastructure and service-based applications that are simply the best out there.

Many web-based companies appreciate the fact that OpSource SaaS can offer them on-demand web application, clearly, OpSource SaaS can give you almost everything you will probably need so you can boost up your sales by performing using great applications in half the time!

But why choose OpSource? Let the C.R.E.C.A. acronym guide you in making the right choice of choosing it as your platform.

C- complete, because everything you will need is addressed in such a software- including hardware, storage, infrastructure, disaster recovery as well as security.

R- it is one hundred percent reliable, because OpSource SaaS has a hundred percent uptime SLA necessary for application and infrastructure, as well as a twenty-four hour support system.

E- it has the potential for extendibility through its ever-growing list of serviceable applications.

C- talk about Compliant- OpenSource SaaS is packed with SAS70, PCI DSS, HPAA, Type II, AppExchange and Sarbanes-Oxley. And finally,

A- Affordable- anyone can get their hands on it with a very attractive pay as you grow type of pricing! With all these and so much more (just waiting for you to try out and be pleasantly surprised at the value-added features), you surely can never go wrong with Opensource SaaS.

SaaS Business Benefits for ISVs and Customers

Information Technology□s aim is to make life simpler and easier. It is clearly evident nowadays that this goal of IT has even exceeded the demands of the public wherein it seems almost everything can be done in just a push of a button. A lot of different processes and procedures were also introduced in the world of business, promising countless benefits not only to the service providers and product developers, but also to the end-users as well. One of these breakthroughs is the Software as a Service (SaaS) model, providing benefits to both independent software vendors (ISVs) and end customers.

SaaS specific benefits to ISVs include the following:
(a) improved customer support and service levels;
(b) shared responsibility for support infrastructure;
(c) more predictable and expected ongoing costs;
(d) lowered risk factors; and
(e) quicker and easier to market.

In addition, partnering with clients gives way for ISVs to concentrate more on developing software applications rather than delivering and operating it, thus enhancing software value. SaaS also fosters closer ties between ISVs and users. Promoting interaction and dialogue will enable ISVs to get feedback on web-based software applications directly from its users.

For clients and customers, SaaS benefits include:
(a) more stable security system- for monitoring network and application attacks or breaches;
(b) faster implementation- easier deployment than traditional software;

(c) more cost-effective- no need to but additional software or hardware, 50% less than traditional systems;

(d) focus more on strategic initiatives- the need for proper delegation is a must; and

(e) lower risk alternative- return on investment is improved and implementation risks are greatly reduced.

Tips for SaaS Companies to Increase ROI

Software as a Service (SaaS) was considered the next best thing when it comes to software automation in the previous years. A lot has been said on how it can benefit users and service providers, which is the reason why a lot of SaaS companies emerged in the past years.

These companies are set to attract small and medium-sized business owners, each of which promises to provide better software solutions at a very low price.

Since competition is stiff and with large companies including Microsoft and Oracle already developing SaaS software, it is indeed a challenge to make your product stand out above the rest. In addition, expect smaller revenue at first due to lower subscription fees. But then again, if your products and services fit the standards of many companies, there will be a brighter future ahead for your SaaS business.

This is the reason why it is a must to design and deliver products differently.

It is a good thing to note though that since SaaS companies make use of web based applications such as the browser, there will be lesser investments in professional services. Operating costs should also drop since a SaaS company can support multiple customers on a single application.

Come to think of it, return on investments can even surpass those of traditional service providers, if everything is done in good taste. Who knows that even large companies may also support your products, so expect a huge difference as far as revenues is concerned. It is always a company's mission to provide innovative products and services to its customers, thus making room for expansion in the years to come.

SaaS Conference- The Details of SaaScon Revealed

It is common to many business enterprises to face challenges and opportunities. It is due to this fact that many innovations on how businesses should be handled properly were introduced. Some have been successful, while some opted to find some more alternatives to produce excellent products and deliver high quality services for the public to enjoy.

To cater for the need to share best practices and learn from success stories of others are just few of the many reasons why conferences are being held. SaaS conferences, for example, are being done in different venues and sponsored by various institutions to find better ways to deliver customer service.

SaaScon is one of these conferences, which will be held on March 25 and 26, 2008 at the Santa Clara Convention Center, Santa Clara, CA. The conference is open for those who are interested to venture on SaaS business, or for those who are planning to hire an ISV and select the best one that suits their business operations.

In this conference, all issues concerning SaaS will be addressed and topics include Measuring Success, Balancing Risks and Rewards, and Taking on Best Practices and Avoiding Pitfalls among others.

Registration is done online, through phone or at the venue itself. Once registration is confirmed, admittance badges will be given to attendees at the registration area.

The stage is welcome to all those who would like to speak; however, this is subject for approval by the SaaScon Management Team. There are also pre-determined speakers, usually coming from event☐s sponsors wherein they will be given a chance to talk for 30 minutes and present their case studies.

For those who are interested to attend, check the web for more updates and details about the SaaScon.

SaaS CRM and its Benefits Over Traditional CRM Applications

Customer Relationship Management (CRM) is a very critical aspect of the business, especially nowadays that more and more companies are reaching out to their customers to determine the products and services that they think would most benefit them.

This is acquired through constant feedback and CRM evaluates these to come up with the best possible solution. There is no other more convenient way to interact with customers other than using the web. This is where Software as a Service (SaaS) comes in.

The concept behind SaaS CRM technology is not that complicated compared to larger systems. This is the reason why it has grown increasingly popular nowadays.

More and more companies, regardless of size, are switching to SaaS CRM to provide business solutions in a more practical and cost-effective manner. SaaS CRM make use of web deployment, which brings about ease of use while eliminating high IT requirements and maintenance costs.

Compared to traditional CRM applications, there are a lot of benefits that the company would get after switching to SaaS CRM. Aside from having lesser worries when it comes to budget, SaaS CRM is also faster to implement company-wide. This is because there is no need to buy additional hardware devices or software applications since it is already made available online.

In addition, data security is much of a concern in most companies. SaaS CRM eliminates this by offering more robust and stable data security measures. These include operating system and database security, user authentication and data encryption among others. Rest assured that confidential information remains secure through these security procedures, providing protection to hazards from the external world.

SaaS Enablement: Delivering Software with Utmost Service

The development of the SaaS, or the Software as a Service as one software application has provided clients with ease and comfort in using a software than paying only for using it and not for owning it.

The driving force behind this application approach is the SasS enablement. When contemplating on which SaaS technology is most useful for a particular application, or what underlying platform is better, the options are many. However, the most useful SaaS enablement is the AE platform (AppExchange) since this is a technology much thinner the very common Netweaver.

Upon deciding the SaaS enablement technology to use, keep two things in mind: Flexibility and Control, and Transparency□.

With flexibility and control, it means determining the creative muscle that users can use with the type of technology opted. With transparency, the experience of the amount of the vendor lock-in is mostly the concern. When the technology becomes more transparent, the lesser its lock-in gets.

A vendor lock-in is relatively similar with becoming a consumer on one monopolized market: a particular technology draws an unfortunate constraint being part of some corral of sorts, which prevents consumers from scrutinizing and finding other more affordable solutions once the quality of the first turns unsatisfactory.

Typically, SaaS is directly associated with more affordable business software that provides consumers with similar benefits from those commercially-licensed software. This is practically the reason why it is important that consumers properly choose the right one that goes well with their preference.

The SaaS enablement should be one factor consumers should focus on. That way, finding that particular software that delivers the best services will not be that mind-boggling to do.

SaaS and ERP- Merging Two Concepts for Business Growth

It always results to a win-win situation if you merge two concepts together that both share the same objectives and goals. This will not only mean good business but satisfied customers as well. Enterprise Resource Planning (ERP) usually applies only to large corporations. The concept behind ERP is that everything will be synchronized by integrating company data, files and records into one single system. This unified database can be accessed by all levels of the organization, including Human Resources, Payroll, Security etc., to promote consistency and accuracy on every process done. Often, ERP requires high maintenance cost, which is the reason why small business owners tend to ignore it. However, recent technology has brought together ERP and Software as a Service (SaaS), making it more convenient for small business to migrate to a fully integrated system.

SaaS functions as a bridge that makes it possible for end users or customers to access a software application anytime anywhere through the internet. All you need to have is a computer, an internet connection, and a web browser and you are all set. This is the reason why an ERP solution built on SaaS is more appropriate for small business due to the fact that it is more cost-effective and it is easier to grasp rather than implementing a much complex system. SaaS ERP solutions are provided by a third party vendor, so make sure that you have chosen the best partner that suits your business. Not all vendors offer the same terms and conditions, which is why it is important to take into consideration all key factors that lead to success of your business venture.

The Many Benefits of SaaS Finance

Most small business establishments have long been using the SaaS finance application and technologies. The benefits of this particular enablement technology approach have clearly shown some positive outcomes, most of which delivering effective software functionalities to various businesses. So what are the benefits of SaaS finance? Read on.

For the consumers. The SaaS finance, or the SaaS application for that matter has no client/server software that needs to be installed nor maintained. It also has a shorter deployment time, just about a few minutes.

And because it is globally available, the SaaS finance can easily be accessed from almost everywhere that has an Internet connection. Additionally, the SaaS also has the service level agreement adherence that effectively report bugs that can easily be fixed even without the rollout overhead. It also has constant and much lesser upgrades, by constantly improving the functionality of the application.

For the provider. The SaaS finance can aggregate the operating environment on the part of the provider. The provider generally owns the domain. Therefore, there is no need to send out technicians to fix software problems.

Also, the provider has complete control in optimizing the infrastructure of the SaaS application's requirements. Furthermore, as providers of SaaS finance application, there is what they call the predictable revenue stream. This means that clients pay the providers on recurring schedules. The providers can also adjust the cycle to better handle the forecasting revenues.

There are really a lot of practical benefits when it comes to the SaaS finance. This explains why this application is mostly preferred my small establishments that still need to have the right enablement technology.

SaaS Growth: How to be Successful in the Industry

The SaaS industry is undeniably growing as more and more developers have realized the success of this business. But in spite of its market potentials, there are still some SaaS vendors that are still struggling to balance the industry growth with is profitability.

SaaS growth can actually be achieved, provided that the web SaaS Company is bent on fueling on the top line while providing bottom line results. Here are some ways on how to have SaaS growth in the world of the SaaS industry.

Balance Growth with Profitability. As with any type of business, the next big thing normally begins with impressive products. However, it is not enough to have a profitable business. Instead, becoming successful especially in the SaaS industry also requires a skilled discipline. By doing so, a more dynamic revenue growth can be achieved while operating at a better profit.

Provide a scalable and cost-effective SaaS Platform. A SaaS growth also needs an impressive but cost effective SaaS platform that provides and accommodates multi-tenant environments.

Also, the performance of the SaaS company, along with the operating reliability and also the growth, all rely on the demand SaaS platform.

For a successful SaaS growth, a SaaS vendor should also expand the product capabilities so as to meet the demands of the market for a more comprehensive management solution.

The more features the SaaS application has, the more likely it is to hit the market. And because this web hosting solution has been provided by a number of web developers already; it has relatively become one web application mostly opted by many.

The Many Benefits of SaaS Hosting

Most small and mid-size business these days are more and more turning on the SaaS hosting. While there are still some that prefer to have those traditional web hosting applications, the SaaS hosting is somehow as efficient and as functional as the ones mostly used by bigger business. So what is a SaaS hosting?

Basically, the SaaS hosting is one software application that is available on the Internet. These web hosting sites are particularly designed to provide shared services to a number of users. Usually, the SaaS hosting is that computer software that is developed and managed by a particular service provider.

Any computer that runs on Mac or Linux or Windows can avail of the SaaS hosting. The computer is primarily connected to an Internet thru a common web browser. This means that users are accessing the SaaS application software thru specific servers instead of just storing them on the computer☐s memory. A SaaS hosting also allows the users to buy more expensive and highly powerful technologies.

Other practical uses of SaaS hosting. Aside from providing small to medium size business firms with web applications far from the traditional web hosting services, there are also some other uses and benefits that one can obtain from the SaaS hosting. With this particular software, clients can access their database anytime, anywhere, provided that there is a reliable Internet connection. Also, the users normally pay only for the model for some small monthly charges, minus those unexpected front costs. The SaaS hosting is also fast, thus running reports in just a matter of seconds.

The birth of the SaaS hosting has truly helped a lot in the IT industry. As more and more clients are satisfied with the performance of this application, developers are even more challenged to provide users with the best possible services.

Some Facts about the SaaS Industry

While most people thought the SaaS is nothing compared with the traditional software, there are actually some things that this software is most noted for. Although some of the SaaS are not that fully-featured just yet, they are flexible enough in meeting the business demands, especially on small to middle-size business scales. Here are some things why the SaaS industry is one system people should consider.

SaaS has long been in the IT industry. Although sounding new, the SaaS industry is already used in a lot of applications. Some popular consumer applications that use the SaaS include MySpace, eBay, YouTube, and iTunes, along with search engines like Yahoo and Google.

SaaS keeps getting better and better. During the early 90□s, the concept is more popularly known as the Application Service Providers or the ASPs, or even called the managed services. Over the years, experts have redesigned the concept with better and more improved services, thus the birth of the SaaS. From broadband connectivity to grid computing, web services and virtualization, the SaaS industry keeps on improving and its practices are continuously maturing.

SaaS is as secured and as reliable as the traditional software. In fact, SaaS is more secured because users need not carry with them their applications elsewhere. Additionally, SaaS projects are more compliant because the vendors are the ones responsible for the tracking of projects and are accountable to a number of customers.

SaaS is suitable for smaller companies. Since SaaS is relatively more affordable than the traditional software, it is more efficient for small to medium-scale businesses.

The SaaS industry has presently continued to hit business and private users alike. With its affordability and high performance, it is no wonder to hear people opting for the SaaS instead of the traditional software.

Achieving the Proper SaaS Infra-structure

There are some distinctive difference between an on-demand SaaS application and the traditional software. Experts say that in order to be a successful SaaS company, there are three must-haves to consider, as far as the SaaS infrastructure is concerned.

The SaaS should be available thru the web. In an SaaS infrastructure, web developers should consider that most of the next generation of clients are not agreeable with something that they cannot easily buy online. It is actually surprising to note that only 13% of SaaS vendors allow online sign up for their applications. A SaaS infrastructure should be available on the web because this is the most effective way to gather and filter possible customers. Also, this can encourage the vendors to assure customers that the applications are web-ready. Additionally, this can also make the software understandable and accessible.

SaaS infrastructure should be more of solutions than components. Normally, most of the conventional software simply provides nothing but a set of tools that users still have to grasp with even before they can finally produce any utility. The SaaS infrastructure has to be more focused not on the toolsets, but on the problems instead in order to have the most comprehensive and best business results.

SaaS infrastructure: Success-based pricing. The proper SaaS infrastructure expects the clients to pay only the application successfully used. This is contrary with what most traditional hosting models go about: charging for the bandwidth and the disk and processor consumption.

Generally, the SaaS infrastructure is far more efficient and useful because of its practicability. This is one reason why small to medium-scale businesses are suited for this type of web hosting application.

SaaS Integration- A Critical Aspect of the SaaS Process

A lot of stories have been written about the different benefits that Software as a Service (SaaS) provides to both service providers and users. Yes, it is true that it is cost effective due to the fact that there is no need to purchase additional software applications and hardware devices just to maintain or support the system. All you need to have is a computer with a browser installed on it, plus an active internet connection. It is indeed more practical than any other software solutions around because it is web-based, which means that you can access it at your own convenience. It is also easier to implement and integrate on your current system. However, not all processes are perfectly executed, thus changing the system to SaaS may look more of a disadvantage.

A good example may happen in small business units. It is indeed recommended that small businesses should switch to SaaS because it will not really take much of the company□s earnings to establish such a system. However, the issue may happen when there is more than one application running via SaaS. To make all of these areas of business perform as a single unit, there is a need to integrate them. But then, the integration process is not that easy. There is a need to do constant error checking and maintenance, thus, defeating the purpose of actually resorting to SaaS as it will require a considerable amount of money to get this done. To resolve such issues, it would be best to use a software application that is intended for SaaS integration. Hiring a professional may also costs big bucks so selecting a software that will work best in integrating the system is therefore necessary.

The Effects of Market Intelligence to SaaS Business

Have you heard about market intelligence? This is a new term to some but to those people who are into the Software as a Service (SaaS) business, they know well what market intelligence is. Market intelligence is the gathering of relevant information to a company□s market. These data are then analyzed to make confident and accurate decisions to determine market penetration strategies, new development metrics, and market opportunities. Market intelligence, with the integration of SaaS, will result to these key benefits.

First, people are getting self-sufficient. This means that everything that you need is already on top of your desk, without really having to contact the company□s IT department for support. Business users can then rely on these data in coming up with the best possible course of action to meet the needs of the business.

The second key benefit would be its cost, specifically on the use of human resources. Since market intelligence will automate the business and remove unnecessary work load, people will now get to work more on the real thing and focus on what needs to be done. Instead of doing redundant work, people are getting more productive, thus saving the company□s valuable money.

Third, automating the processes done through market intelligence will make the job a lot easier, especially for marketers. Since the information at hand is already converted into something that they used to seeing, the time to generate reports will be lesser than expected. As a result, better marketing decisions are produced with higher competitive analyses in terms of quality. Truly, this will be a win-win situation for the company and its customers as well.

The Right Approach in SaaS Marketing

In SaaS marketing, most successful companies that deal in this industry often think of themselves not as a software company that sells software on demand. Rather, they consider themselves as a Web company that has business users that access their services over the Internet.

In order to effectively start a successful SaaS business, understanding the right approaches to SaaS marketing is imperative. Here are some tips.

SaaS vendors should think about their identities. SaaS vendors should understand that it is important to reconsider their base offerings. Software vendors must provide SaaS applications that generally emulate the varied consumer Web sites in such a way that they are designed and distributed to obtain success, rather than those that follow the more traditional enterprise software.

SaaS companies should be updated.. Traditional software companies normally look at the long term benefits of their products. But with SaaS, this web application can easily add newer features either monthly or quarterly. It can also develop a larger number of platforms, thus making it more iterative. Additionally, Web application developers of SaaS are generally free to explore and focus application capabilities as well as the user experience.

SaaS marketing takes a lot of effort in order to succeed. Most SaaS vendors often feel the need for newer developments to reach out to clients, although not so many people appreciate these changes. SaaS marketing is basically all about providing the best web applications at a more meager price range. With so many SaaS vendors at present, there is only one thing SaaS developers should focus on: to attract users and not to sell to customers. After the user base has been developed, the focus then extends to elaborating the product, this time providing additional features that are often useful to clients.

SaaS News: Keeping Updated with the Latest in Trends

The SaaS is one of today☐s most successful trends in the world of software development. The SaaS solutions have solved a lot of problems that most traditional software is facing which includes highly expensive upfront license fees, access issues, and long time implementations. Over the next couple of years, the SaaS is expected to become more pervasive in all areas of the software market.

In keeping with the latest trends, the SaaS news is helpful so that investors and web developers can fully understand how the SaaS industry goes and properly assess the impact in the world of software development.

Based from the latest SaaS news, the market size of this industry is expected to reach up to a hundred billion dollars, although this will be a gradual evolution. The desktop applications, as well as the enterprise application markets are seen to stand at about twenty-four billions and sixty-five billion dollars respectively. The system infrastructure for SaaS also includes network security and desktop applications, virtualization, and back up.

Additionally, the SaaS news also stated that there is a hundred percent of desktop applications that have successfully delivered on demand SaaS solutions over time, thus seen to obtain about thirty-eight billion dollars opportunity by 2010. As for the enterprise applications, about ten percent of all the data can not be accessed on demand as per governmental mandates. This means to say that government and international data deemed as confidential can not be stored off-premise nor be co-mingled.

The SaaS news is indeed one of the most effective methods to gather information about the latest trends in the world of the SaaS industry. Learn and read more about them now.

Understanding the Benefits of the SaaS Platform

The SaaS platform is one or a collection of computer programs that collectively acts as the host of the computer applications that is residing on it. Aside from that, the SaaS platform is also responsible for tenancy partitioning, scaling, monitoring and metering, and distributing services.

Tenancy Partitioning- In general, applications that are written in one tenant fashion have little or even no function in serving a number of customers. One example is a specific application database. If the database is designed to cater only to a single customer, then this prevents other customers from storing their data in that same particular database. Additionally, the execution of an application cannot possibly be partitioned nor shared by customers.

Scaling- An SaaS application intentionally aggregate the demands for all users and customers into a single virtual or physical location. In any SaaS application, therefore, being able to support the said aggregation is an important requirement. So as to achieve scaling, the SaaS application should be designed in a manner conducive to scaling, while still being able to support the required auxiliary pieces.

Monitoring and Metering- SaaS applications are also required to meter and then monitor the usage from the data as well as the execution standpoints. Generally, this is closely related with the monetization and the scaling models. Also, most of these applications are extracted into platform layers wherein the platforms then become responsible for the metering of the user and the tenant usage, while monitoring the system events as well.

Distributing Services- SaaS platforms are responsible in distributing services into the system to achieve the tasks of performing business logics.

Companies that distribute SaaS platforms these days have effectively introduced varied services to the market but generally, they have followed the basic principals mentioned above.

How to Go About in SaaS Pricing

When it comes to providing the right SaaS pricing for buyers, a software publisher is often faced with the dilemma of doing the right pricing, without compromising the existing license sales.

Every software developer and publisher should be able to balance their current product rates and their SaaS pricing, otherwise, they might risk a great loss on their market shares. So what should vendors do in order to provide the most amenable SaaS pricing?

Product Bundling. Whether the product relates to television programming, software designing or software distributing, product bundling is often the most proven and effective strategy to achieve varied price points that come from different market segments.

In distributing software-related product bundles, the first thing to do is to carefully distinguish the SaaS service bundles and the traditional licensed products. It is also helpful to vary the features on each of the bundle.

This can help the software vendors in creating segment specific offerings with different price ranges. Also, doing this could potentially distinguish the licensed products' rates from the SaaS pricing.

At present, software developers and vendors are starting to increase their SaaS pricing.

However, users should not be bothered about this because the SaaS services are relatively improving. The SaaS industry has positively extended into more diverse areas, providing better and automated business services.

Expensive or not, the SaaS pricing is one thing buyers should fully understand. After all, the SaaS industry at present has continued to provide on-demand revolution, creating software that performs better in the operations of automated business services.

Advantages of SaaS Project Time and Tracking Management

Unanet, Journyx and Clockware are some of the companies that provide project management software under the Software as a Service (SaaS) delivery model, specifically in project time management and project tracking field.

Some of these companies solely provide software using the SaaS model only, while some integrates usage of licensed software and SaaS applications. This means that the user will first have to test and access the software through the internet and once it is working perfectly, the local IT personnel can then install the full version of it on the computer.

However, not all companies provide such level of service. This is the reason why it is very important to ask your SaaS provider questions on how you can implement the full potential of the software application for ease and speed of usage.

Customer support is also one of the things that should be taken into consideration as the software application should be made available 24 by 7 and potential problems might arise during certain times. Asking such critical questions is crucial to the success of the business.

SaaS project time management and tacking solutions have the following advantages:
(a) reduces much risk because there is no need to acquire new software;
(b) removes much of the cost to maintain and operate business functions;

(c) enables users to accurately predict ongoing expenses because budget for IT is tightened and further analyzed;

(d) paves the way in improving the quality of products and services offered due to ongoing ties between the vendor and user; and

(e) provides the flexibility of changing usage commitments when the need arises.

Microsoft's Approach to SaaS Project Implementation

Microsoft is by far the company to beat when it comes to producing new software applications that the market truly needs. An industry leader in certification programs, operating systems, office software tools and internet products, Microsoft continues to strive to dominate other areas of the IT world.

When something becomes a hit, expect that Microsoft will develop its own. One of these innovations is Microsoft's version of Software as a Service (SaaS) application, also known as the Microsoft SaaS On-Ramp Program.

With a lot of programs developed under its name, Microsoft still aims to cater to all levels of the business.

It is a fact that big companies can afford to implement traditional on premise solutions, but for small and mid-sized businesses, this is much of a concern. SaaS is the solution to this, making on demand applications easier to reach on the web at a very affordable price.

Now that the Microsoft SaaS On-Ramp Program is here, independent service vendors (ISVs) can now take advantage of obtaining Windows and SQL Server 2005 at a 0 rate for 30 days without any upfront payment. Once applications are up and running, Microsoft will then charge them for a monthly subscription that is usage based, meaning how much will be billed☐ depends on ☐how much is used?☐

As an ISV, first consider three things if you are interested to apply for the Microsoft SaaS On-Ramp program.

First, ask yourself ☐Is this the program that I want to pursue on having?☐

Second, ☐Are the benefits that the Microsoft SaaS On-Ramp Program provides suit your business?

Third, ☐Is it cost-effective?☐ After your assessment, subscribe to the Microsoft SaaS On-Ramp program now.

The Difference You'll Get by Subscribing to a SaaS Provider

The secret behind the success of a certain software solution or process lies on its implementation. Just like in the world of Software as a Service (SaaS). It is in the hands of the SaaS provider on how to automate the processes and methodologies needed in carrying out business operations.

This is the reason why more and more companies are considering in subscribing to a SaaS provider and see the difference it can create as compared to on-premise solutions. Some of these variations in terms of service and implementation are enumerated below:

(a)   Financial differences. Yes it is known to all that on-premise solutions produce more revenues than SaaS applications. This is also due to the fact that it takes lesser cost to produce SaaS applications. There is no need for any additional hardware and software tools to maintain and operate business functions when you are subscribed to a SaaS provider.

(b)   Development differences. The development process behind SaaS providers is instant since they immediately see what actually is working well and what is not.

(c)   Technical differences. This is very obvious since SaaS is designed for multi-tenancy. This means that a single application program can be accessed by several users in an instant through the web browser that runs an internet connection while keeping every data transmitted secure and protected.

(d)   Marketing differences. SaaS providers allow free trial uses to their prospective clients. Usually, customers have 30 days to decide if they want to keep the SaaS service or not. Subscription to SaaS vendors are mostly done online that often focus on marketing gratification.

SaaS Revenue to Increase Tremendously in Year 2010

What do you think is the reason why big companies nowadays such as Microsoft, Oracle, SAP, IBM and even Symantec have all considered developing and releasing Software as a Service (SaaS) applications, not only intended for small businesses but for huge corporations as well?

Some companies may say that they are just developing SaaS software solutions to render services to more people or simply to tighten the competition and give more people options to choose from.

This is actually a win-win situation for consumers but certainly becomes a threat to SaaS vendors such as Salesforce.com, which has dominated the SaaS market for a lot of years now.

But then again, it is obviously the increase in revenue of SaaS vendors that has paved the way for this sudden switch. Gartner Inc., a Stamford Connecticut- based research firm has reported on the 10th of August, 2007 that the worldwide SaaS revenue within enterprise software markets is projected to surpass the US$ 5.1 billion mark in 2007.

This is a huge 21% increase to the revenue earned in 2006. Gartner Inc. further indicated that SaaS worldwide revenue will even reach as high as US$ 11.5 billion by the year 2011 due to the large number of companies switching to SaaS software applications.

Limited upfront investment in staffing and capital, rapid deployment and ease of use coupled with the reduction in maintenance and support for software management are indeed more than enough to make SaaS as the most desirable alternative to many on-premise software solution. These reasons keep the wheel running for SaaS vendors despite of the competition imposed by huge software companies.

The challenge to develop more reliable and consistent SaaS software applications will be the driving force of these vendors in obtaining worldwide success and recognition.

The Result of the Growth in SaaS Sales

Since the demand for Software as a Service (SaaS) continues to grow, more and more software vendors are realizing the significance of developing SaaS delivery software solutions.

A huge portion of the market belongs to small and medium-sized businesses, though huge corporations are also considering the switch. Though not accepted at first, SaaS has become one of the fastest growing industries today.

The search for a better alternative to on-premise software applications has been made possible through years of hard work and determination from the efforts made by SaaS vendors.

Because of this renewed passion for SaaS that software vendors are seeing huge numbers in terms of sales and usage. Among small businesses (SMBs) alone, a Connecticut-based research firm known as the Saugatuck Technology Inc. has reported an increase in SaaS adoption from 9% in the year 2006 to 27% in the year 2007.

Though there is an increase in the number of SMB subscribers, there are still some who were reportedly dissatisfied from the services that they got from certain SaaS vendors. S

ome claim that ease of usage and installation, and low cost make SaaS appealing than traditional on-premise applications, issues about flexibility and security are still being raised. Another research firm named Gartner Inc. has reported in 2007 that 45% out of the 307 US SMBs said that they do not trust the data coming from third party companies such as SaaS vendors. A very low 7% said otherwise.

This is indeed an ongoing challenge for SaaS vendors to prove to the world the integrity of their products. It is because of these issues that SaaS vendors are holding an annual SaaS Economic Summit to form new software strategies and evaluate current practices.

The Ups and Downs of Salesforce as a SaaS Provider

One of the leading software companies that have been proven in developing the best Software as a Service (SaaS) software solutions to many businesses is Salesforce.

Though Salesforce has remained focused more in introducing innovations primarily to small businesses (SMBs) from the beginning, still it is making a mark and creating an appeal to medium sized businesses and large companies

In mid-2005 alone, Salesforce proclaimed its largest deal with 5,000 seats at Merill Lynch, followed by the Salesforce Sandbox company preview later that year.

Salesforce Sandbox is a hosted training and testing application and was set for a major release in winter of 2006. Salesforce applications continue to grow and in late 2006, it introduced an online billing and marketing service for certain companies that demand such online applications.

At that time as well, Salesforce reported to have 27,000 subscribers with more than 400 application offerings on its AppExchange, Salesforce application directory. In spring of 2007, Salesforce released ContentExchange, a new application to manage documents. Salesforce even borrowed from Web 2.0 to let users to organize content and added Apex Content to move towards a full SaaS platform.

But then again, success has been known to be coupled with a lot of challenges. Downtimes and outages in Salesforce made bad news and even irate customers as well. This happened in late 2005 until the early days of 2006. This issue resulted to bringing SLA to the front position for customer protection.

Salesforce has yet to recover from such issues. But then again, it does not matter if the SaaS market has opened its doors to new players. With a lot of competition around, Salesforce is here to stay& for good.

The Undying Issue Regarding SaaS Security

With the development of a lot of on demand applications nowadays, it is indeed a fact that Software as a Service or SaaS has come a very long way from its conception in the ☐90s. Though at first SaaS providers are having difficulties convincing customers to shift from traditional on-premise software applications into a hosted one, this has changed as companies, regardless of size, have realized the business sense and concept behind it that they have eventually accepted and adapted it in to their own system. This is real good news to independent software vendors (ISVs) as more and more companies are seeking for their services.

An increase in awareness of the various benefits of SaaS is one of the reasons why many resorts to seeking the best ISV to host applications to their web site. Looking back, it is always a matter of security why some companies are a bit hesitant about the idea of dumping critical and confidential data into an anonymous server that belongs to a third party vendor. However, this has changed in recent years as SaaS applications are proven to be more stable and secure with the association of different security measures such as data encryption, user authentication and database security.

Indeed, customers have soon realized that privacy and security concerns can be associated with any application, either in-house or on-demand. However, it is still best to ask questions to learn more about the different security measures that SaaS vendors can offer to your business. Select the one that will truly protect company information since risk in security is difficult to take for granted.

Win the Hearts of SMBs Through SaaS Integration

More practical and cost effective: these are just two of the many reasons why small business (SMB) owners are convinced to consider Software as a Service or SaaS in automating business processes and operations.

It is because of SMBs that even software industry giants such as Microsoft and IBM has joined the bandwagon, seeking on-demand solutions to customers making SaaS as the best alternative to traditional on-premise software applications.

For SaaS vendors to be more appealing to SMBs, here are some of the things that they should keep in mind. First, they should concentrate on speed of use, rather than ease of use.

Yes, it is important to find more convenient ways on how users can easily make use of the software. But then again, speed is something that should also be considered so that more work can be processed at any given time.

Second, invest on security. Learning to apply the recent breakthroughs in protecting customer data will attract more and more potential SMB clients in the future.

Third, access to information should be available at all times. It is a fact that customers may encounter downtimes as far as access to the internet is concerned; therefore it is necessary that customers have the ability to work offline and have basic navigation options to save loss time.

Lastly, it is a must to communicate well to customers the benefits of SaaS so as to avoid false expectations. There should be a balance between software and service. While it is important to concentrate on developing new on-demand software solutions, it is also important to provide customer support for better implementation of the different methodologies concerning SaaS.

SaaS Solution Your Way to Success

Do you still remember those days when you are right in front of a hundred new licensed software installation disks and hardware devices, thinking which one will suit your budget and meet the minimum system requirements for your computer? Do you still buy the idea of having to call your employees at the office to make sure that every file is backed up to prevent data loss from power outage?

How about go to the nearest computer shop and buy the recent software patches and upgrades just to maintain high standards when it comes to business operations? Thank heavens and you can leave all those things behind. If you are in the process of putting up a business or currently having one, you may want to consider implementing Software as a Service (SaaS) software solutions to ease all your worries in an instant.

Yes, this one is true. All you need to have is a computer with an internet connection and you are all set. There is no need to buy extra hardware or software. Everything is right in front of you, thanks to your very reliable browser.

The concept is simple& you take care of your business and your SaaS vendor will take care all critical information flowing on your system. What's good about this software solution is that your valuable data can be accessed anytime you want. In addition, all records and information are kept on a very secure server, so rest assured that these are stored in a safe zone. Lastly, subscribing to a SaaS solution provider is so affordable. So think about it. Subscribe now and let your SaaS vendor do the rest for you.

The Need to Switch to SaaS Solutions

Information Technology (IT) is the driving force that makes it easier for people to develop new ideas and trends that will eventually hit the market. Such examples include Apple's iPOD, Sony's Play Station Portable (PSP) and Microsoft's Personal Computer (PC). This has changed people's lives dramatically as the demand for new breakthroughs in technology becomes a part of every day living, making life a lot simpler and more convenient.

The same thing happens with software applications: from an in-house software that can only be accessed on a single computer can now be accessed by a lot of users through the use of the internet. This has been made possible by the introduction of Software as a Service (SaaS), a delivery model that keeps on innovating as new demands and breakthroughs are being introduced on today's generation of software applications.

A lot of these changes have something to do with globalization. This does not only create grounds for new market opportunities, but also globalization has paved the way in developing stiff competitions between companies. This also resulted to the modernization of today's world, with the introduction of new ideas that can definitely make a mark in the IT industry. The growing dependence on companies to deliver state of the art SaaS solutions to obtain business objectives has increasingly dominated the software market. This responsibility has been brought about by the sudden changes in the demands of the public. Nowadays, business professionals are relying more on online services, thus creating a positive consumer experience. Thus, the SaaS generation is here to stay, hoping that someday everything can be done in just a mere push of a button.

SaaS Strategy- The Basic Steps toward Successful SaaS Implementation

With this day and age, a lot of businesses nowadays are into business automation. This means that every little process is done on the computer. But then again, the need to buy licensed software applications and additional hardware devices may seem to appear a bit tough, especially when you are running out of valuable money. This scenario is very common to small and medium-sized businesses, wherein every penny counts. The good thing is that the responsibility of handling every business process and storing critical business information can now be transferred to a third party software application vendor. This strategy is known as Software as a Service (SaaS) and for years, this has been the known alternative to on-premise software applications.

Software experts have devised a step by step basic guide on the proper implementation of SaaS to every business venture. First, you have to assess your business and recognize the needs of your customers. A clear understanding of the concept behind the SaaS strategy is also important that will result to having well-defined objectives and avoiding false expectations.

Second, form a team of individuals that will carry out day to day business work loads. Designing of infrastructure components is also done on this stage. See to it that you consult with your team to purchase only the ones that your business really needs.

Lastly, it is now time to select your Internet Service Provider and SaaS vendor. It is appropriate to take into consideration your budget and system infrastructure in determining the best among them. Work with somebody that you truly trust for the proper implementation and deployment of SaaS processes to your business.

SaaS Summit- When SaaS Professionas Meet for Tomorrow's Software Industry

Do you want to know more about the latest strategies and best practices nowadays concerning Software as a Service or SaaS? If yes, then you may want to attend the SaaS Economics Summit and SLAM Conference 2008, which will be held both held at the Sheraton Gateway Hotel in San Francisco, California on April 3 and 4, 2008. These two events were made possible through the efforts of Software Business, which happens to be the same organizer for the foremost industry event called Software Business 2008.

The SLAM Conference 2008 and SaaS Economics Summit have joined forces to increase the awareness of the software industry about the latest breakthroughs and technologies enveloping the world of SaaS, with testimonies from the various software companies that continue to dominate the market. The SLAM Conference 2008 will area of concerns are the following:
   (a) licensing, pricing and sales programs;
   (b) branding and marketing;
   (c) alliance and partnering programs;
   (d) customer support;
   (e) market opportunities;
   (f) international product strategies; and
   (g) service and product development.

Another reason for the expansion of the event is to talk about all the issues that surround SaaS and how these can be addressed in a more strategic manner. Such issues include the following key subject areas:
   (a) revenue recognition;

(b) sales and exit strategies;

(c) raising capital;

(d) tax and accounting practice:

(e) financial management for operations;

(f) benchmarking and market analysis of SaaS companies;

(g) managing licenses and subscriptions;

(h) sales compensation models and

 (i) case studies of leading SaaS vendors.

The Changes in SaaS Trends- Are You Ready For It?

Trend in software development is extremely difficult to project. There are times wherein a certain software application dominates the market and before you know it, after a while a new and improved version of it will be developed. The only difference here is that this time, a separate vendor will be responsible in releasing the new software. The only advantage it can create is for end users wherein they get the services that they want, and at same time, at an even lower cost. The similar case happened with the development of Software as a Service (SaaS) application solutions to most businesses nowadays.

At first, the trend is that SaaS is the only one that customers can count on to provide software automation processes to their business, no matter how small or large it is. This is actually the proposed alternative for costly on-premise software applications. Return on Investment may be obtained easier using in-house solutions rather than on-demand, but then again, the costs it take to maintain such operation is also critical to the business.

But then again, there came a time wherein many doubted the capabilities of SaaS, especially in terms of data security. This has triggered many businesses to combine SaaS solutions to on-premise applications. Because of this, big software companies even ventured on improving SaaS implementation, making it appear as if it works like on-premise applications. This is what technology is all about. It brings a whole new different world where collaboration of ideas is needed to provide better services to people. This is also one of the reasons why the world keeps on rolling, as new software solutions are yet to be introduced in the years to come.

SaaS Vendors and Their Critical Role to Business Automation

The software vendor plays a very critical role in the success of the proper implementation and delivery of Software as a Service or SaaS. The SaaS vendor is the one making it possible for users to access relevant business information on the internet by using on-demand software applications. Managing the operation of software applications, as well as developing new strategies to provide software solutions for ease of use on the part of the user are also some of the responsibilities of the SaaS vendor.

The SaaS delivery model is also cost effective, wherein the customer does not need to buy any additional hardware tools or software applications. For as long as there is access to the internet, the user can easily monitor the system, as well as make changes or generate reports whenever necessary. It is because of these reasons why SaaS applications are considered more economical than the usual commercially licensed and internally operated on-premise applications.

Acceptance to SaaS was not that easy. There are a lot of questions in people's minds that made it harder for them to accept the SaaS delivery model at first. However, SaaS applications kept on improving every year through the combined efforts of various SaaS vendors. Concerns about the potential risks in security are all wiped out with the integration of data encryption and user authentication. These are some of the security measures that users can get, ensuring the protection of very critical business information from being accessed by outside threats. Keeping the flame alive by introducing more features will eventually result to better service and is therefore necessary to earn the loyalty and respect of clients. Indeed SaaS vendors have made great progress

When Industry Giants Aim to Dominate Over SaaS Vendors

Software as a Service or SaaS is indeed the one of the fastest growing businesses today, as more and more players, including software industry giants, are jumping into the SaaS vendor bandwagon. This is because they have sought the importance of on demand applications as excellent alternative to traditional on premise software tools.

Nowadays, SaaS does not only cater to small and mid-sized businesses, but large companies are seeking for it as well.

Thus, these sudden shifts in software development strategy pose as a threat to SaaS pioneers. This is not actually something new in the world of sales and marketing. Competition gets even tougher when consumers have more options to choose from, and the best solution provider of course will remain standing.

The quest to dominate the SaaS market is still ongoing, especially now that Microsoft, IBM, Oracle and SAP, have joined in to provide better service solutions. The advantage of these companies is that they have the resources to come up with SaaS software applications with a wide range of functionalities, as compared to leading SaaS vendors such as Salesforce.

This market opportunity has paved the way for the development and implementation of innovations and breakthroughs to the SaaS industry, making it more convenient to expecting consumers.

With such challenge imposed by additional software vendors, SaaS pioneers must consider reinventing their own application, not only to better serve their current subscribers, but attract new ones as well. Large software industries may have the technology, but SaaS pioneers have their own track records and experience as they have fully established the significance of SaaS for the past years.

It is a must to revisit strategies and perform best practices that continue to have an appeal to the SaaS market.

Staying Afloat with SaaS

SaaS or software as a service has a lot of great benefits for those who are interested in adopting it into their businesses. According to software as a service enthusiast, the best features of SaaS would its network-based access, management and commercial availability of its software activities. These are great because all are easily managed from key locations instead of poring over each on in all of their customers' websites. It is also great because of the attractive element of web-based accessibility so that customers can remotely access their applications on line anytime, anywhere.

The type of web application delivery of SaaS is similar to the one to many models than a one to one model. This also includes software as a service architecture, pricing, management a partnering characteristics that also include many centralized updating of features ☐ and such eliminates the need to download additional patches and software upgrades.

The software as service applications are priced on a pay per use basis ☐ sometimes with additional fees for more storage and extra bandwidth, but generally the price is said to be quite affordable for individual users and small- to medium-scaled businesses. As such, the revenue streams of software as a service is lower than the more traditional licensing fees of old software ☐ but its main selling point is the total lack of need for software maintenance ☐ which greatly reduces the hassles in any business. With a relatively cheap price tag, a host of useful and easily accessible applications and ease of use, software as a service or SaaS is definitely the way to stay afloat in the software technology industry.

SaaS 2.0- An Exciting New Offering That Will Surely Blow You Away

While the current trend now is putting a number version after most products and software out on the market today (like 2.0, for example), not all will perform better than the previous offering. In fact, some people have gotten so used to the version this and version that up-to-the-minute offerings that more often than not has had many a consumer go 'ho-hum, what's new?'. Thankfully, the same cannot be said regarding SaaS 2.0. Everyone ought to get ready for the second version of SaaS- as 2.0 signifies all the good things that await those who get their hands on it.

SaaS 2.0 is a very secure software that allows many businesses to experience a more efficient process and work flow. Clearly, SaaS 2.0 goes above and beyond what we know business drives to be today. Add to that its low-cost price, and you have got one neat system that will not cause you a leg and an arm. Simply put, SaaS 2.0 is all about being able to help its many users- novices and professionals alike- transform their business processes and allow them to generate better sales and better business performance.

Because of this and so much more, do not expect SaaS 2.0 to be a mere rehash of the first offering. Your business will surely benefit much from it, and when you find yourself leaving your competitors in the dust you will know that you have made the right decision. Try out SaaS 2.0 today and experience it for yourself!

A Stress-Free Way of Managing Accounting with SaaS

Any business will need accounting applications to manage not just the company's financial profile, but also to ensure that the business is performing up to standards. Thankfully, SaaS accounting can help many professionals take stock of their company without having to outsource for extra help. Basically, the accounting application of SaaS is just a part that makes up the entire software itself. It seamlessly syncs up with other aspects of the software such as Calendar, automation of sales forces, management of contacts, customer relationship management and other things that are an integral part of any business. A SaaS accounting software has comprehensive accounting applications and it is designed in such a way that small businesses can have real-time knowledge regarding the financial activities of their company and so much more.

Accounting aficionados will excited to learn that SaaS accounting applications now include new and useful features such as easy to use set up guides so it will be easy for businesses to create as well as manage their own information while backing up their business data in a regular manner. And for those who are tasked with such an important and vital responsibility, it is definitely a joy to hear and learn about a great new way of managing financial information without having to develop extra big eye bags overnight in the process. Many small business owners have been known to say that their start-up companies definitely need the skill to manage both their accounting and financial activities without going through the hassle of purchasing expensive material, hiring someone to install it and managing the workload in a traditional manner. For them, SaaS accounting is definitely the best news that they have heard in a long time.

The Best Move You Can Make Now: SaaS Adoption

In these recent times, a lot of companies and seen the light and have made the move to adapt to change. Part of this adaptation is ensuring that their businesses are using software as a service, or SaaS in their day to day transactions. Recent studies show that software as a service adoption has become the rising trend in businesses, especially those that are web-related or of the technological kind. Both big and small companies have been making the move towards SaaS adoption simply because they know that if they do not, they will be left in the dust and will find their businesses losing their profit flow. SaaS adoption will allow them to create business solutions in half the time and have new implementations enacted quickly.

Another thing that has lured many businesses towards SaaS adoption is their interest in using the wide range of applications that are part and parcel of the package. More than half of companies all over the Internet have indicated an interest in exploring the possibility of using SaaS for their businesses, and a lot of them have actually made the move to do so.

Because of SaaS adoption, the use of software as a service has ceased to become a minority in the business industry □ instead, it has become a beacon of light that signifies a company's commitment towards improving themselves in order to serve the market better. This is clearly echoed by early adopters of SaaS, who have been enjoying it for a long time.

What Do I Need To Know About SaaS Applications?

Basically, any software you can get through the SaaS is already considered an SaaS application in itself. Some areas in IT where SaaS can prove to be a viable application model are CRM (Customer Relationship Management), Human Resources, Video Conferencing, Email, and Accounting.

It can be said that SaaS solutions (or SaaS applications) can be considered web-native applications because their technologies were made especially to adapt to browsers.

SaaS allows enterprises to gain access to commercial software applications (not customized solutions) through network-based access to and proper management of such software.

SaaS software is managed in a centralized way rather than as on-site applications available at every user site. The user can get the SaaS software using the Internet as the software delivery infrastructure.

SaaS software also usually adheres to a one-to-many form of architecture in its form of application delivery. This applies to the management, partnering, pricing, and architecture aspects of the SaaS software as well.

When you seek out SaaS software, you may find that each SaaS application will be priced per user, and may require that your organization have a minimal number of users before you can get SaaS service. If you want additional bandwidth plus storage capacity, you may need to pay extra too. This allows SaaS developers to earn lower revenue than that earned by traditional licensed software developers and vendors but which is more predictable and recurring. Thus, in a competitive business environment, a SaaS host may be able to earn more consistent income than that earned by traditional software vendors and developers.

Some Thoughtful Considerations for SaaS Applications

A lot of companies have been pondering over a very important decision they have to make for the sake of their business: how do they know which and how to apply SaaS applications in order to come up with the best results? Basically, a penny for their thoughts will yield two additional questions that will help them arrive at the right answer. One, which SaaS applications are well suited to the particular needs of the company? And two, will such applications be able to support the company in a manner that is cost-effective and will continue to perform in the long term?

While it will not be instantaneous to answer such questions regarding SaaS applications, it will definitely be to the 'ponderer's benefit to study other people's past mistakes with SaaS applications that are on-premise. They should know that SaaS applications have a wide range of applicability for companies that are both big and small.

And since SaaS applications are widely being used by small to medium-sized and large businesses, these applications have proven to be reliable. They are able to give companies the security they need in their businesses as compared to other applications. The important thing is to look at the businesses' objectives and match it with the SaaS applications so that they can come up with the competitive edge. Yet another thing to consider in SaaS applications is the impact of such an application to the direct experience of the customers to the different channels of the business. SaaS applications will change the face of the business, and it is important to select one that will allow the customers to react to it in a positive manner.

SaaS Architecture: The Simple Foundation That Launched Many Successful Businesses

SaaS architecture is here to stay □ but only for those who truly understand what SaaS architecture is and demands of its users. Because of the entire buzz created by the proponents of software as a service, it is no wonder that people have begun considering adapting SaaS architecture to their businesses □ both big and small.

In SaaS architecture, the make up of the entire system is based on a foundation of service-oriented computation. It must be important for the business to note that while SaaS architecture helps make the business itself work to its fullest potential, its design and execution keeps the consumers in mind as the end recipient of such meticulous work and planning.

The system that flows through SaaS architecture is but a simple operation of sorts. It allows the user to seamlessly navigate through the model by being able to easily access control and maintain security at all times. SaaS architecture is also designed to provide a sense of control in order management and provisioning tasks. Management and the monitoring of SLA is also a breeze with software as a service architecture. Furthermore, the metering, billing and extensive customer support of SaaS architecture will certainly make a lot of mouths go □Oh!□ and □Wow!□ in pleasant surprise.

Indeed, SaaS architecture is one refreshing breakthrough in the world of business and technology as it is able to increase business productivity, provide excellent client service and give companies a sense of trust in a system that will never fail them.

Powerful Solutions of SaaS-based Software

Many leading providers of SaaS-based web applications and solutions are on a race to provide the best possible support for many businesses. A lot of SaaS-based applications are now incorporating new technologies to make their packages much more attractive, such as integration with business suites that are specifically designed for many small and mid-sized businesses. The meaning and significance behind the modification of SaaS-based solutions is that a single architecture that is low cost but fully functional will generate more fans. Clearly, SaaS-based integrated business solutions will allow any businesses to perform well past their previous expectations. Founded on a unique framework and special delivery method, SaaS-based web solutions ensures complete integration of data across all the departments in all organizations of any business. SaaS-based applications will allow a company's employees to work with their business data and allow its seamless transfer efficiently.

SaaS-based web solutions are focused on helping the consumers increase their sales and boost their performance by allowing their businesses to perform at optimum levels. They leverage the most leading edge technologies out on the market and thus are able to come up with a solution that connects all vital aspects of the business. Such secure and enterprise-like applications will definitely allow any company that has made the sound decision to use SaaS-based applications to become a leader □ or at the very least, a competitive player in the modern business arena. Using SaaS based software for the sake of the consumers world wide is definitely a very good news.

Wonderful Benefits Brought About by SaaS

SaaS has a lot of great benefits for people who have made the right choice to utilize it. Consumers will be very pleased to know that software, as a service will allow them to make their work and business very efficient and enhance their total work production.

For one thing, SaaS does not require any client and server software installation or maintenance.

This save you a lot of time because you can get to work right away without needing to leaf through eight hundred plus pages worth of implementation guides. SaaS also has a shorter deployment time, and we are talking mere minutes here, as opposed to other phased implementation schemes that can actually take months to deploy.

Customers and clients will truly appreciate its global availability because let us face it, who would not want to experience functionality that is available on the Internet, easily and efficiently?

It service level agreement or SLA has a very efficient application so there are lesser bugs. Using software as a service application will mean very constant but easily manageable upgrades, so you have the latest in innovation all the time.

This can be due to the fact that the SaaS provider has you in mind- always wanting to improve your software application experience. The changes are so miniscule that the upgrades can actually save you a lot of time and money- and all companies want that. What is more, it can also help redistribute your information technology software budget by being able to outsource software functionality to the provider- allowing the enterprise to realize a savings in cost when it comes to the requirements of infrastructure.

Billing Considerations for SaaS Efficiency

A lot of vendors that offer software as a service or SaaS have a different kind of billing and revenue process of management that will allow them to go beyond the capabilities of their present financial infrastructure. As everyone knows, pricing can be highly variable and will also include some bundled services supports and upgrades. Every single account will require a monthly bill that can accurately present charges for the past transactions, the current services and some future subscriptions as well. One will definitely need a single platform that will be able to drive both billing and accounting needs straight from the customer contract and the usage data.

What is important is to integrate the metering feeds, because this is essential in order to operate and the desired scale. The revenue accounting policies must always be enforced throughout the entire process. If this does not happen, then the revenue items (most especially the overage fees) will be likely to fall through.

The single platform for SaaS billing will provide several key benefits for the users. For one, it can allow the unification of all financial data and system operations. It also has the capacity to tailor bill the presentation to their customer's unique preferences. Single platform billing will allow them to easily manage many complex pricing schedules, as well as automating revenue and the expense accounting. This type of SaaS billing platform is easy to use when it comes to integrating the metering with other types of usage tracking systems, enhance the initiatives of compliance and heighten the company's insight when it comes to business performance.

SaaS Blogs are Here to Stay

If you still have not noticed, the current buzzword in today's business- especially in information technology- is software as a service, or SaaS for short. This has been the most important technological revolution of our time to date, because it allowed a lot of businesses- especially those done on the internet- to create services at a much more efficient pace. Which is why it does not come as a surprise why there are so many SaaS blogs popping up everywhere.

These SaaS blogs can serve many purposes. One purpose is to, unsurprisingly, promote the many benefits of using software as a system in different types of businesses.

People are always crawling □round the internet looking for feedback regarding new products and services, and one great way to look for such is through blogs that offer a comprehensive review on technology.

SaaS blogs can also help people with the way their software as a service application works. Because we can create, we can innovate. And when we can innovate, we have the capacity to share with others a knowledge that is for the betterment of systems. Tips, tricks and great advice regarding SaaS can be found in different SaaS blogs all over the internet. Being able to share different tips with others is good, because only good things can come out as a result.

SaaS blogs can also serve as a buying guide for many prospective customers and clients of SaaS applications. Indeed, SaaS blogs have a lot of benefits for both customers and providers alike!

What Do SaaS Blogs Contain?

SaaS blogs are basically blog sites that contain opinions by the owners about the Software-as-a-service (or SaaS application) which is generally used by corporations to gain access to much-needed applications via the API of the SaaS. SaaS blogs are necessary in a way because they help SaaS developers to learn about any flaws or loopholes in the system they created. But since SaaS blogs are written based on the opinions of people, you must learn to distinguish between objectively-written SaaS blogs and those that are simply trash talk.

One topic about the SaaS field that you may encounter in the blogs is about how SaaS should be priced and what factors should be considered when computing for SaaS pricing. The first factor SaaS developers should consider is the periodic base costs. They then add on upgrades that will drive up the cost some more. However, SaaS pricing should not be that hard because the SaaS model is more predictable than that of other IT services- which means SaaS pricing is equally predictable.

Another topic that may come up is whether SaaS should be offered only to your existing customers or to new prospects as well. It is generally accepted that old customers are easier to sell your IT services to than any new faces in your prospects list. However, SaaS ought to be also sold to new prospects to generate additional or new revenue streams. This is because old customers inevitably run out of needs for you to serve or funds to buy your new SaaS IT services.

Thoughtful Considerations for Better SaaS Business Models

There are many speculations going on regarding whether or not the IT industry is going to transfer to a new SaaS business model operations. There is an existing trend to provide software as a service while billing payments over time, and we have witnessed an emergence in the usage of such. There are many economic pressures that prompt people to see the new SaaS business model appear very much attractive, both for makes of software and the corresponding enterprises.

They have seen the sale price of average license tumbling down bit by bit, the stagnation of volumes and eventual consolidation in the industry. A change in the business model will definitely rest on a few elements. Some of these elements or considerations include a much lower cost of software ownership, the characteristic of flexibility to alter the usage commitment as the business circumstances currently evolve, more economically wise business cases, faster rollout time and accurate computation and processing of the information technology budgets for better returns on investment.

A lot of SaaS business model hosting services has developed an increased awareness and a heightened mindshare with regard to raising the issue of the SaaS business model□s suitability for a host of other applications. Applications that are good for outsourcing will definitely require a reasonable fit for being such a service. The business model will need to consider this and a lot of other things in order to create more widespread acceptance and utility among the software industry and information technology-capable populace.

The Value of Capital in the SaaS World

Research indicates that a lot of capital is required in order to help make a software as a service business rise between fifty to seventy percent higher than the former perpetual license model. These percentages are driven by what is called the pay as you go model of business. Capital is needed, yes, but what drives success tenfold will be a wise understanding of how to work one's way around one's SaaS capital.

The best way to do this is to commit to three or five times more cash than any traditional lenders. The SaaS capital will recognize the value in the business model enough to allow you to monetize the future value of your unbilled bookings. It must also consider the facilities that one needs to grow in order to make the bookings grow as well. Negative amortization will help eliminate needs for any future equities. And what is more, when you borrow only what you need you are engaging in a more cost-effective way to make your business grow.

Keep in mind that for most lenders, they do not require any equity infusion before the funding. They consider your situations and predicaments, and work best to provide you with the SaaS capital that you need (and not because you have tons of money stashed away in the bank). It also offers no warrants, so you do not end up paying too much for your balance. These companies want you to know that they are one hundred percent focus on your software as a service needs, and this is enough for you to trust them just the way that they trust you to make your business grow with the help of their SaaS capital.

How an SaaS Company Works for You

SaaS companies revolutionize the way other industries design their products, the way they deliver them and the intricacies that underlie the entire work process. Software as a service companies work hard to make customers highly satisfied, as is easily reflected in their income statements. The selling point of many SaaS companies? An easy payment scheme that included up front license fees as well as professional service fees- annuity-like and locked into either two or four year contracts.

SaaS companies work to improve the cost of revenues in software as a service, since this will require a small amount of investment in their professional services- a point that can be attributed to the increased deployment of web-based delivery. A software as a service company can be considered fully developed if it is able to produce gross margins that are comparable to the traditional models of software licensing, minus the margin drag of many professional services. Furthermore, their operating expenses will also drop, mainly because the companies have the means to support as many customers as they can on just a single shared application and system.

Currently, this software as a system opportunity that most SaaS companies are looking into for big potential is still in its infancy stages. The great thing about this is that based on research, the performance of the two or three best companies are top notch, easily turning software as a service companies in a very favorable light. And for providers and customers alike, this is great news □ for business, for communication, for transactions and more.

Understanding the Need for SaaS Conferences

First off, what is SaaS? SaaS is categorized as a software application delivery model, which simply means you use the Internet to gain access to different software applications. The SaaS allows SaaS software providers to do software maintenance, and software upgrades; eliminate bugs from your system; and gain a faster capacity to supply various products to market while assuring functionality.

Thus, it may be said that SaaS conferences allow SaaS software providers to inform their peers and the public about the importance of SaaS to customers and to the companies offering SaaS themselves.

One issue that software developers and software users alike may be concerned about when entering or offering the SaaS business is security and operational threats. One point of view about this is that SaaS may endanger the Information Technology operations of the clients using it. But this is countered by another school of thought that says SaaS may actually be able to boost security for the clients through the SaaS business model. Nowadays, SaaS vendors have been able to improve the programming interface through customization plus publication.

There are some trends which have enhanced acceptance of SaaS such as: many people now own their own computers (either desktops or laptops); standardization of applications is possible; customization has become possible as well within basic function parameters; the improved reliability of Web systems; security has become more transparent yet secure at the same time. If SaaS keeps improving as a software application delivery model, then most likely more software developers will try to offer SaaS in the future. And that would make for an interesting future for SaaS, for those interested in following future events.

The Tricky Bits of SaaS Contracts

For many decision makers of software and those in charge of purchasing business software, software as a service can be both novel and familiar at the same time. The underlying principles of contract negotiation have not been changed just because there is new trend that has been added to the word list.

As it turns out, you will still need to figure out how many seats you will require for any given application in order to determine the contract term (and additionally, seeking out better discounts). Generally, a software as a service contract will charge X amount of dollar every month (or on a quarterly basis) for Y number of end users.

If you are willing to negotiate, here are some timely tips to help you come up with the best contract for your SaaS applications. When you negotiate, make sure that you are able to differentiate between configuration and customization. You need to remember that your contract spells out what most vendors consider configuration and what they also mean by customization. Keep in mind that the former is usually free while the latter is somewhat expensive. If you do not get to have clear look at this, your supplier might dish out some customization fees that you might get surprised about. Along this line, make sure you look at the stability of the provider. This is highly important because at some point you will need to consolidate. Therefore, you will need an exit strategy as well as the skill to negotiate a form of transition support.

Defining SaaS: A Closer Look

Everyone's all a-buzz about software as a service, but when you really get down to it, what does it all mean? Basically, software as a service is a type of software application model of delivery wherein a vendor services web-based customers by coming up with a web-native software application that is hosted and operated independently of through third party applications. The customers do not provide a fee for owning the actual software itself □ rather they pay for its usage. They use SaaS by means of an API that is accessible over the internet and are often written using web-based services. The term SaaS for software as a service has been established as the industry preferred one, as it has replaced the previous terms Application Service Provider (or ASP) and On-Demand.

These give clients access to network based software and provides them with a whole range of opportunities for customization and management. The software activities that they manage from key locations allow the customers remote access to them via Internet. It can be a single instance model, or a multi-tenant architecture, depending on the needs of the client and the structure and nature of their company. The software use package takes into consideration a lot of elements that include architecture, partnering, pricing, and characteristics of management that are both centralized when it comes to updating features, which then preclude the need to download upgrades as well as patches. Sometimes additional fees are necessary depending on the number of users who wish to avail of the service.

The Growing Trend in SaaS Delivery

Today the entire market for total business applications is able to do software as a service (or SaaS) delivery across the vast Internet marketplace as a means of service □ and a healthy one at that as well. The demand for it is getting healthier and healthier, continuously and steadily feeding on what marketing and research analysts all say will most likely be an extremely steady diet of newer, stronger and more revived subscriptions not and in the future.

This ever growing brand of SaaS delivery is what some may look at as the latter-day turn of events on the different types of existing hosted applications model that unfortunately fell out of favor during the gloomy years of the dot-com bust. Then again, while many businesses in the Internet industry can still find ways to locate many vendors who are willing to host their enterprise resource planning (or ERP) and other types of applications off-site, the undeniable attractiveness of the software as a service delivery model is that all of these businesses combined are enabled to use the application tap in the same was as the software, having for themselves a shared type of model that can allow providers to decrease the cost of its ownership.

The applications are so attractive and generate so much attention when they are delivered as a service (or on-demand as well) that two years ago one research firm confidently predicted that they will slowly but surely dominate around twenty five percent of the business software market, with a target end to date of 2011.

Considerations for Optimum SaaS Development

A lot of the giants in the software technology industry are leveraging the delivery model of SaaS in order to further increase their leaps in growth, responsiveness and agility. Software as a service is able to allow such innovators to markedly reduce their market and profitability times. While this is happening, the model is also doing much to increase SaaS development's penchant for productivity and total efficiency.

This SaaS development is good news for the customers, as it translates into a lower price in the total cost of SaaS application ownership. It is also easy to implement and has a fast time to increase in value. Therefore, one can say that thanks to SaaS development, SaaS has truly become the choice business model for a lot of software companies throughout the world.

It is very important to consider the development of new SaaS platforms because it can redefine the relationship you have with your customers.

It can make the relationship a lot more efficient, creating bigger and better transactions in half the time. But before you dream this up, you need to consider the SaaS challenge and its ability to seamlessly integrate in your business set up.

You need to ask yourself if you can get the process of your product development to support the rapid fast development cycles of SaaS. You should also consider your readiness for shorter cycle times, which invariable creates more decisions that are highly effective.

Think of how you can systemically capture- as well as assess and put together user feedback into SaaS development. Consider if you have enough visibility going on in both product development and the delivery process. And finally, will you be able to have a common storage for the artifacts of the development process? These are some of the questions you should ask.

The Establishment of SaaS Directories: Everyone Benefits

A lot of consulting companies nowadays have seen the light and have seriously put in much time and effort into integrating software as a service (or SaaS) directory into their systems. These and a lot more different types of companies are currently joining the software as a service bandwagon, hell bent on launching important avenues in technology industry such as on line SaaS directories of providers. A lot of these companies truly want to familiarize themselves with the types of applications that can be found and are delivered in a SaaS model, but most of them do not know where to start the great search. Using search engines can truly make them expend effort in a problematic way, and a lot of application exchange websites are limited in terms of their wealth of knowledge.

The best solution to their little predicament is to watch out for launching of websites that serve as SaaS directories. Some of these websites are here to serve the software as a service provider, while some focus their attention to the needs of managed service providers (or MSPs). A lot of companies that are currently concentrating on developing SaaS directories will also soon be offering the tried and tested method of □yellow paging□ the model as an effort to enhance the listing. For a small fee, customers and clients can have access to software as a service companies and SaaS companies can unlock the door to msp companies as well. This definitely sounds like a great way to form new business relationships over the Internet, much to everyone's benefit.

Ease Up Your Productivity with SaaS Document Management

Having a bit of trouble? Baffled because you do not know where to start? Well, now you can breathe! Start providing solutions to your document management woes without having to go through the hassles of installing an application software on your own. There are a lot of software as a service (or SaaS) document management applications that are freely available out there to help you and your organization manage your files and increase your work time without needed to invest in software and hardware, as well as hiring technology staff just to be able to do this. SaaS document management can provide you with extremely high speed access to all your files and all your documents from anywhere in the world - minus the hassles of accessing it via model web browser. It also has very easy to use web interfaces!

The unique combination of SaaS and open source all rolled into one complete document management process means that you will not get locked into a vendor's SaaS document management source code, because it is freely downloadable. You can get started right away without needing to give up front investment- thereby lowering your risks. The applications will allow you to get immediate access and allows you to easily evaluate the software, thus lowering your risk of implementation. The total cost of ownership is also lower because you do not need to invest in any hardware equipment, or hiring out service of the maintenance of such hardware. You also do not need to hire a software staff just to manage a data center, because everything is commanded by yourself!

The SaaS gov relationship in the SaaS industry

Even though many software vendors are now venturing into the SaaS market, one market still remains difficult for SaaS vendors to penetrate with a marked degree of success □ and that market is the US federal agency business.

SaaS translates to Software as a service which is believed to bring more cost savings to end users (as opposed to buying software outright.) The main reason barring US federal agencies from patronizing the SaaS business model is the usual government concern about threats to security and privacy. The current mindset in the government bureaucracy and absence of pertinent data standards also hinders adoption of SaaS by the US government.

It might be said that SaaS software vendors may need to have courage to tap into the US federal government agency market, and that courage should be matched by the courage of the US federal procurement officer who will stake his or her reputation on the SaaS solution he or she gets for the federal agency. In government, failure is never an option and can lead to the procurement officer losing his or her job.

Another reason SaaS gov solutions may be hard to sell to US federal government is that usually SaaS is a pay-as-you-go system. US government agencies have to be able to predict expenses because that is how government agencies function.

Still, if SaaS developers can manage to address all these concerns and give appropriate solutions, then SaaS may be a viable solution for the US government as it faces attrition and smaller budgets.

Bullish Performance of the SaaS Mod

Developing software and delivering it to consumers as a service is a new innovation in the software market. SaaS mod or software as service model actually started getting the attention of technology specialists and consumers just recently. It is a novel way of selling computer applications to a wide consumer base.

Software as a service incorporates two factors in the technology equation and those are advance computer software and Internet technology.

Individuals or companies in need of a particular program can utilize it through the web browser. It eliminates the use of on-site installations and local servers to host the application. The program can be accessed remotely because the vendor provides everything, from software, remote hosts, to technical support. The SaaS model brings to end users all the convenience in using the program.

Start up companies can benefit greatly from the SaaS model. Because of the characteristics unique to SaaS, start up companies can reduce their initial capitalization requirement and save on operational costs concerning their information technology needs.

They also get the maximum benefit of having a fully operational computer application and a 24/7 technical support at a cost that could be considered peanuts.

SaaS technology at present primarily services small and medium sized companies.

But this sector of the software industry has been showing vigorous growth in the past years.

This could be interpreted as a very positive reaction of the market to software services. If trends continue, the SaaS model could replace the established software distribution model. This possibility is actually not far from reality.

SaaS Model Trailblazing New Path for the Software Industry

Why buy a license when you can just rent the technology? This has been the catch slogan of many software vendors trying to sell the SaaS model. And it is true. Software as a service is a business model that rents out a computer application using the Internet as a platform for the delivery of the service. It is an innovative service which significantly reduces the expenses of end users in terms of buying licenses for the software and setting up the necessary IT infrastructure to run the application.

A lot of software companies today are jumping on the SaaS bandwagon. Many computer applications have been enabled in order to run the SaaS way. This segment of the software industry has been growing for the last few years in terms of increasing sales and customer base. On demand software for individual and personal use as well as business and enterprise software have been developed to meet the demands of the market.

Businesses, especially start up companies, are utilizing SaaS for their basic computing needs. The model reduces their initial investments because SaaS eliminated the need to set up a full IT division together with its concomitant technology architecture. Businesses are using SaaS to run their customer relations management, automation of sales and marketing division, and human resources management. These are only some of the vital functions that SaaS companies can handle. Top-caliber ASPs are already including inventory control and management and corporate financials to their software deployment. That is why the SaaS model has been gaining loyal customers and paid subscribers.

Marketing the Solution in SaaS ppt and other Rich Media

Application service providers have been aggressively marketing software as service to lots of businesses. Campaigns to increase the users of software services involve the use traditional and rich media marketing tools. Many SaaS ppt or Powerpoint Presentations, documents, banner ads, and white papers have been produced in order to explain the benefits of software as a service model.

The marketing drive has been paying off because market trends point to the increasing migration of small and medium sized enterprises from traditional on-site software solutions to SaaS based deployment of computing needs. The success is primarily hedged on the fact that software hosting solutions offer up-front and long term benefits especially in terms of reducing corporate overhead expenses and flexibility in using a hosted service.

Through the use of software services, companies eliminated the need to set up their own servers and to recruit technician and specialist needed to maintain the infrastructure. Aside from the cost saving benefits of SaaS, companies can enjoy organizational flexibility because different divisions if located separately can still function and access the company's computing applications. This is because SaaS uses the web as its delivery point and anyone who has a browser and Internet connection can use the application provided by SaaS companies.

The increasing number of SaaS model users and the robust operations of application service providers show that this type of software business has the potential to make big advances in the IT industry. In fact, even established and traditional software vendors have started to offer some of their software using the SaaS model.

Ensuring Quality SaaS Service Means Market Dominance

A critical point in ensuring the success of a SaaS service company is its capability to comply with the high expectation demanded by consumers. End users will naturally expect and demand that the software provided by application service providers will be readily available whenever and wherever they want to use it.

This means that SaaS companies must ensure that uptimes should always be in top running condition at all times. To achieve this, a SaaS company that wants to be known as a top caliber service provider must utilize every advance technology infrastructures at their disposal. Redundant power supplies and powerful data servers must always be live 24 hours a day on a 7 day work week.

They must also recruit diligent and competent IT professionals and technicians that can monitor the activities of the software and the infrastructures that run it. Trouble shooting should be as prompt as possible and upgrades should be delivered by software developers in order to effectively fix different bugs in the software.

It is also a known market fact that customers demand efficient, competent, and ready support for the software that they use. Failure in this area can result to unfavorable customer relationships and could lead to customer migration to other SaaS companies. In order to avoid these dark scenarios, a SaaS company must ensure a working customer relationship management program.

The SaaS industry today thrives in a very competitive environment. Software giants and institutional IT companies have started to implement SaaS services to get a piece of this lucrative market. It would be beneficial for SaaS start up companies to ensure quality in every level of the service to ensure success.

Enhancing Customer Flexibility in Using SaaS Software

A good thing about SaaS software is its inherent capability to fully function as a regular web-based application. Typical SaaS software utilizes Web 2.0 functionality. This competence makes the program interactive and opens the possibility of costumer to costumer interaction.

Interconnectivity with other software users can create a healthy community of interested and involved individuals. An end user may customize the software to suit individual needs without touching the core codes of the program. Because of greater interaction between users, the customized development can be shared to other users thus giving impetus to further refinement of the application.

This also sits well with the SaaS company and its software developers. They can cut costs in terms of developing simple customization. SaaS companies can also easily spot popular and useful customization created by its users which can lead to system upgrades and new patches. This saves SaaS companies of valuable research time.

The Web 2.0 utilization of SaaS software separates it from on-site, locally installed computer programs. On-site software will take longer time to develop and upgrades can happen after months or even years of use. This is unfavorable for a very fluid and fast developing market such as the software industry. On the other hand, SaaS software upgrades can take shorter time to develop and customers can instantly benefit from the development. This instant gratification of customer needs has made SaaS software more competitive versus the traditional on-site programs.

The potential of SaaS software in delivering the needed software solutions to diverse groups and companies has trebled overtime. This is due to the fact that SaaS software allows users to take control of the program at their levels and effectively share it with other users.

SaaS vs ASP. What's the Difference?

Many software vendors are already selling their products online. Software as a Service and the Application Service Provider have often been mixed and interchanged. SaaS vs ASP really have major differences in the way software is being availed by the customer.

ASP basically covers traditional application. Traditional applications are applications that were originally not designed for the internet but were later modified to fit the online market.

Early online companies utilized ASP and the power of the internet to allow traditional programs to be accessed by customers and clients instead of them physically installing it on-site.

This type of delivery drastically changed the software market because ASPs were offering a pay-as-you-need-it type of pricing scheme.

The software industry was greatly shaken because now, even without much money, a person or a company could already afford a subscription-type model base. SaaS vs ASP was still non-existent during the earlier days of the internet. The ASP modified existing applications that were not meant for web-access and offered them for download on the web at very affordable prices.

With ASP, software was regarded as a service application instead of a product purchase and SaaS was born because of ASP□s limitations based on the legacy software development. While there may be many overlapping definitions of SaaS vs ASP, SaaS became the new model of software delivery in every type of software that were used.

With SaaS, the software service was paid in a subscription basis rather than on a single payment license.

SaaS vs ASP both are software available on-demand and on the internet and both are capable of instant activation.

SaaS Definition in Wiki

According to wiki, Software as a Service also known as SaaS is a popular software application in the internet and has the ability to make deployment to customers easier.

This will decrease the customer costs and this will also help developers in supporting their clients with one product. Clients are not tasked to pay and own it but rather for using it. SaaS wiki defined it as linked with business software and is commonly considered as an inexpensive method for companies to get the similar benefits and advantages of software available in the market. Usually this commercially licensed software can incur difficulties and can cost a lot of initial charges.

According to wiki SaaS has several kinds of software that fits SaaS application. This will benefit clients who have computing needs and less interest in software operation. This is a convenient application for customers. SaaS has been successful in initiating the application in various areas such as Video Conferencing, Customer Relations Management, Accounting, Email and Human Resources. Unlike the older applications in the web, SaaS was made to control web technologies like browser.

SaaS, as wiki defines it, provides network access to available software in the market. With this application, the activities are organized in one location. This also makes it easier for clients to use applications even in distant locations by using the internet. The price of SaaS applications are computed on per user basis. This depends on the minimum amount of users. This usually provides extra fees for storage and bandwidth.

SaaS Wikipedia Gives Several Results

When people go online and type SaaS Wikipedia, they are greeted with several results. Wikipedia is an online, web-based, multilingual encyclopedia project that is accessible to anyone who has an online connection. Wiki means collaborative while the □pedia□ part is from the word encyclopedia. The articles inside Wikipedia are free of charge and usually contain accurate information about any subject.

SaaS or Software as a service is an internet-based, commercially available software that can be managed online. A central host manages the software so that the user is always assured of an updated software each and every time. It is a pay-as-you-use type of service that even allows a try-before-you-buy or money-back guarantee to the user.

As mentioned in the first paragraph, SaaS Wikipedia will give an individual several choices about the term SaaS. If a person types SaaS Wikipedia, he will be shown a page containing different articles about SaaS. There is a place called SaaS in Switzerland and inside SaaS, there are 5 communes and valleys that contain SaaS.

There are also different types of abbreviations for SaaS when the words SaaS Wikipedia are typed. According to Wikipedia, SaaS is also an abbreviation for Student Awards Agency for Scotland, Seattle Academy of Arts & Sciences, Salla Allahu Alayhi wa Sallam (which is □Peace be upon him□ in Arabic), the South Australian Ambulance Service and the Software as a Service.

So when researching for Software as a Service in Wikipedia, the words □SaaS Wikipedia□ should not be confused with other SaaS or SAAS terms.

Service Oriented Architecture: Creating a Virtual Global Village

Having interconnectivity and interoperability using wide networks could be the simplest description for service oriented architecture. Essentially, service oriented architecture is a set of specific services that can communicate or coordinate activities with each other. For example, an online banking system program can communicate and interconnect with the user's forex trading account during fund transfers. Any transaction arising from these web based computer applications can be recorded in the user's financial planning software reflecting income earned on bank deposits or expenses incurred during withdrawal transactions.

Basically, that is how service oriented architecture works. It provides a platform for users to synchronize and organize their data computing activities in real time. It can also be used as a tool to speed up transactions with other web based services by integrating different information.

Service oriented architecture is a very useful web function. It gives consumers the capability to acquire different services from various providers using only a computer console, an internet connection, and a service application. The consumer can request a service from the server of a provider and in turn the service provider gives back a response to the request. The development of this technology has made modern computers virtual offices.

Service oriented architecture can be used for simple data input, transfer, and retrieval. However, it can be used also for complex processes and business computing especially if the enterprise operates a global network. Tighter integration of individual business units using different software application can be made possible using service oriented architecture platforms.

The Soa SaaS Marriage of Convenience

Good software service providers should enable their applications through services oriented architecture in order to deliver suites of applications to multitude of users. The soa SaaS combination is a marriage of convenience for the two technologies to deliver computer programs under a multi-tenant environment.

Early application services providers failed in their ventures to deliver SaaS because of issues involving software scalability and flexibility. Back then, service providers deployed computer programs without foreseeing the necessary technological architectures needed to support the program. The results were devastating when the ASP bubble exploded because it cannot meet the demands of the market.

New SaaS players have learned from this lesson and have integrated services oriented architecture as a building block of hosted software and applications. This resolved the problem of software scalability and flexibility which are the main concern of the software market. Today software services can be deployed seamlessly in multi-user, multi-tenant environments and the application can be used on different platforms. The needed architecture is there to effectively host the delivery of the programs.

The use of services oriented architectures also allowed SaaS enabled programs to have a little degree of customization and integration with other software solutions. This sits well with the consumers which needed a software suite that can function on different environments and can communicate with other computer programs.

The success of new SaaS providers can be attributed to the wise integration of software hosting to service architectures. A SaaS provider could avoid the fate of ASP companies in the nineties if it builds its hosted applications on reliable service architectures.

An Introduction to the Software as a service (or SaaS) concept

Software as a service used to be known mainly as the Application Service Provider or the On-Demand service- and yes, it is actually a service because customers pay to get to use a web-native software application (as opposed to purchasing the software outright for their personal use.) Software as a service is now more commonly known though as just SaaS throughout the industry.

To get to use the web-native software application, the customer has to rely on a source code interface called an API (or application programming interface.) An example of an API that the public might be familiar with is the Play Station 2 official API from the Sony company which helped Sony to maintain control over whoever could access the official API. Sony restricted use of its official API to just licensed developers of the Play Station 2 gadget which in turn allowed Sony to determine who could write games for the Play Station 2. Not only does this allow Sony to impose quality control policies on both the Play Station 2 and Play Station 2 games, but Sony can monitor any opportunities to license new technologies based on its own product.

On the other hand, the API of Microsoft is generally accessible by the public to allow new software to be developed based on the Windows OS platform. This is the more open type of publishing policy when it comes to the API source code interface.

Other widely-used samples of API are those that belong to MediaWiki API, YouTube API, Google Maps API, Simple DirectMedia Layer (SDL), DirectX for Microsoft Windows, the OpenGL cross-platform 3D graphics API, the Macintosh OS Carbon, the Macintosh OS Cocoa, the ASPI employed for SCSI device interfacing, the Java Platform for the Standard Edition API and for the Enterprise Edition API, the SUS or Single Unix Specification Windows API, and the PC BIOS call interface.

Software as a Service SaaS: Promising Better Services

Software as a service or SaaS is not new in the IT business. This type of software business model has seen better days in the early part of 1990. It was called ASPs then or application services providers. The limited success of ASPs was due mainly to its inability to deliver the expectations of the market which rested primarily on software reliability. Back then, software service providers focused their attention on building data centers and main frames that can host the applications. Software development was sacrificed. The expensive build up of hardware was not complemented by expected profitability which resulted to huge losses.

Today, there is renewed activity in this segment of the software industry. The market has been reacting positively to the new software services providers. This is due to improvements and advances in software development which now gives the consumer increased flexibility and customization. The bullishness of the SaaS business model is now the hottest topic in the IT industry. More start up SaaS companies are emerging offering innovative and user-friendly software. Some of the most successful SaaS providers are deploying their applications to numerous businesses and enterprises.

The impact of software as service is beginning to be felt in the business world. Some enterprises have been adopting the SaaS model as a solution for their computing needs. This is especially true in the fields of customer relationship and human resources. More complex business processes however are being enabled to work in the SaaS environment. These developments contributed to the increasing popularity of software services among technology analysts, technicians, and end consumers.

Software as Service Signals a New Boom for Businesses

The advent of software as service has unleashed the potential of new businesses to make significant headway in competing with other established companies.

Software as service, also known as Software as a Service or SaaS is a fairly new technology. It incorporates advances in software development, computer hardware technology, and web interconnectivity.

Application service providers deploy software and computer programs to numerous clients in order to provide reliable business process and data computing management. Service providers also provide hardware that is needed to process different information from numerous customers. Secure data storage and allocation of sufficient bandwidth are also important components of software as service business model.

End users and technology consumers on the other hand benefit from SaaS by having a specific computer program which can be operated virtually.

The program will not rely on local installation and this will ease the burden of setting up expensive hardware and eliminates the very costly registration for software licensing. Companies which operate globally will be spared of setting up different server stations.

Company processes and data needs can be easily acquired using standard Internet connections. This can significantly lower over head costs and savings of companies can be invested in other productive ventures.

Software as service has come a long way from its inception in the 1990s. Application service providers are getting savvier as computer technology advances. As a result, more and more companies are shifting their software deployment solutions from locally installed computer applications to the purely web based software as service model.

Great Strides in Software Hosting Technology

Software hosting is not a new technology. It has been around for many years now and many Internet users, whether individuals, non-profit group, or corporations, have benefited from it. Software hosting companies and providers offer numerous software solutions for different computing needs.

Today, almost every computer application needs can be serviced by software hosting businesses. Software hosting providers can give reliable service to a wide range of clients.

Consumers can get software designed for specific needs like email marketing, community forum and bulletin boards, web site building, finance planning, corporate accounting, enterprise resource planning, and many more.

Software hosting could be a free service if providers use it to complement other premium services. In most cases however, software hosting can be enjoyed by subscribing to the service provider and paying a regular or one time payment for its use.

Paid or free, software hosting is a good tool for computer users who wish to deploy a computer program without local installation. Users can also get up to date patches and upgrades of the software usually at no cost. Software hosting companies can also provide real time technical support for their clients using modern internet communication technologies such as VoiP, web conferencing, instant messaging, and online tutorials.

The impact of software hosting has been felt not just by individual computer users but also by online and brick and mortar businesses. The utilization of software using web based interfaces greatly helped companies and organization in simplifying and streamlining their software solution needs.

Software Service: Delivering the Ultimate Computing Solution

The tremendous popularity of delivered software service has gripped the Internet even software provider giants have joined the fray in developing the technology. Software service or more popularly known as software as a service (SaaS) is an ingenious model of providing a fully functional software application that can be used immediately over the Internet by end users.

Today, SaaS is primarily being used for business computing and data storage needs. It is viewed by many as a cost effective way of deploying enterprise-wide software solution. The service eliminates costly investments in purchasing application software licenses and setting up the necessary hardware and infrastructure to run the application.

The technology which started in early 1990s put together the best aspects of software development and cutting edge Internet connections. Businesses can now take advantage of cheap, reliable and secure data management giving chief executives and IT specialists more time to focus their efforts on the business□ core processes and competencies.

The market for software service continues to enjoy increasing acceptability among business owners and corporations. In the near future, it is not surprising if it can match the stand alone software or suites in terms of market leadership and consumer use.

Software as service is a good option for businesses that have enormous computing requirements but do not possess the capability to develop and support the necessary applications environment. In other words, SaaS provides businesses convenience and flexibility in handling their essential data and process management. With less investment but more computing power, the potential for growth could be amplified.

op SaaS Companies

To become a top SaaS vendor, companies must get away from the traditional enterprise software and offer SaaS applications that are truly consumer based.

They should be able to develop a focus on adapting with the changing online environment as well as concentrate their marketing efforts on attracting more customers. Yes, one-shot, big-time deals may give these companies the instant cash but only a constant flow of customers assure them of a steady inflow of income.

Top SaaS companies always develop their products on the basis of user experience of their software applications. Unlike traditional software companies that make major releases after a few years, SaaS companies add newer features and capabilities to their products on a regular basis. Top SaaS companies usually make releases on a quarterly or yearly basis because they are not constrained on any platform.

Top SaaS companies also constantly have a feedback feature that can monitor and ask users how they find the product, what are its best features, its weaknesses and many more. Being a web-focused SaaS company will surely allow the business to only concentrate on the programming of their application and its interaction with the customers.

Closing a big transaction was the old way of dealing software. Traditional software companies usually focus only on selling their products to dealers.

But top SaaS companies know that in order to succeed, they should be able to attract more users to their products instead of just selling their software to customers. Having more users will assure them that their customer base will increase and the use of their product will continue well beyond the second, third, and fourth version.

Why Are Top SaaS Companies Upbeat about the Potential of SaaS?

SaaS is formally classified as an IT service which permits companies that pay monthly fees for the API access to get various applications through the Internet. When SaaS (or software as a service) is used, venture capital fund managers tend to favor investing into SaaS companies. This may explain why, although 2007 was not a good year for investments into IT companies as a whole, top SaaS companies might still be feeling optimistic that they have a better future this 2008 due to interest from venture capital funds.

Software vendors might be able to get more consistent revenues while reducing their research and development costs if they tap into the potential of SaaS (rather than stay dependent on packaged software products.)

It is perceived that complicated enterprise software applications might not be as lucrative as the SaaS application for any companies that are aiming for renewed growth in the IT industry, especially if these vendors are aiming their enterprise software application at Fortune 500 firms.

One good SaaS business model that investors might want to investigate is made up of SaaS applications that work for clients who are not interested in major systems integration applications. The ease with which SaaS applications can be used by many users without resorting to vast IT implementation projects is a major selling point in the favor of SaaS applications.

Another reason SaaS is doing well is because even a small corporate player can get the functionality of a much bigger corporate player if SaaS is employed compared to other systems.

Utility Computing Services can Slash IT Budget

Common utilities like electricity, water and telephone services are comparable to utility computing. In fact, the term utility has been used to describe this particular service in order to show similarities with other consumer-based utilities.

Utility computing works on per use and per demand basis. Customers will pay the service providers only if they use the computing utility. Service providers literally rents out their computing and data storage services and charges users based on the length or duration of the use. This is also known as metered computing or metered computing services.

Utility computing can cut data computing expenses of companies. It is a step ahead of fixed payment for other on demand services. Because companies pay only the service providers whenever the need arises, they can easily control their computing expenses. On lean days, companies may opt out from the service only utilizing it when there is a surge in computing demands. Companies can also save a lot because it would be unnecessary for them to invest in purchasing lots of computer console, server main frames, software, and of course, personnel to run the system. L a company has to do is to activate the account with a service provider and outsource their computing tasks.

On demand services like utility computing is becoming a popular service for most consumers. Other applications using pay per use principle has been applied to other online services such as pay per view, video on demand, pay per download, web access, and Internet hosting

Utility computing is a very innovative service. This kind of business model enhances the maximization of limited company resources for a very low related cost in investment and overhead expenses.

What is SaaS? SaaS in Plain English

What is SaaS? Software as a service or SaaS has become so widely used today that its meaning and definition has been stretched and modified to suit every vendors marketing needs. Fortunately, there are some top SaaS companies that try to give a more specific answer when asked what is SaaS to them.

So what is SaaS? Sadly, SaaS will never be properly defined because there will always be new definitions, sub-definitions as well as twists and loopholes in the definitions of SaaS. But to make it a bit easier for an individual to understand what SaaS is, four basic characteristics have to be present in order for a company to truly be called an SaaS company: it should be multi-tenacity, the services should be shared, it should have a feedback mechanism, and most important of all, it should be a pay-as-you-use only service.

What is SaaS when it comes to multi-tenacity and shared services? SaaS is a multi-tenant software that allows different customers, from single individuals to large corporations, to run the same program.

There may be basic differences here and there but the program should basically be the same. SaaS should be able to link up to other services that are available online like third-party programs that have partnered with the company.

For example, if an SaaS company offers web statistics service, it should also be able to access other programs that enable it to monitor the activities of the website, user database, and many others.

What is SaaS when it comes to feedback mechanisms and pay-as-you-use service? SaaS companies should always have a feedback mechanism in place so that customers, and even the software, are able to immediately report problems or difficulties encountered as the program was used.

This makes it easier for updates to be made. It should also be a type of program that does not bind the customer to the service for a long period of time.

Reasons Why SaaS is the Future for Online Service

There are many reasons why SaaS or software as a service is so popular nowadays. And they really are very simple: the multi-tenacity layers of its stack, the pay-as-you need it pricing scheme, its shareware feature where payment is not immediately demanded, the vendor responsibility for the management and infrastructure and application, and the regular updates that are automatic in most cases. The customer-focused and customer- driven approach is why SaaS is the transaction of choice for many people.

The method of delivering the product is also one of the reasons why SaaS is very much suited for small and medium-sized companies. Some large enterprises have also started some pilot projects on SaaS because of its easy, no-fuss payment system as well as its very flexible license agreements. Without the need for an initial cash outlay, the products can be tried and tested before a company can actually purchase the product. And even after the product has already been purchased, the customer-focused approach of the vendors makes upgrades and updates a part of the product feature. This is why SaaS has been gaining popularity to many large corporations also.

So there really is no reason why SaaS should not be trusted by individuals, small and medium businesses and even large corporations. Although there may be concerns about security, privacy and data control, because the data is hosted by a company that has all the data from other customers also. There are also some SaaS companies that have very limited or non-existent service level agreements. But all in all, the reason why SaaS is a better choice still outweighs the cons.

005.3 BLO

A/L

Printed in the United Kingdom by
Lightning Source UK Ltd., Milton Keynes
139197UK00001B/60/P